Fully Equipped

Dr. Ruth M. Wilson

Edited by Claude R. Royston

BK Royston Publishing LLC
Jeffersonville, IN

BK Royston Publishing
P. O. Box 4321
Jeffersonville, IN 47131
502-802-5385
http://bkroystonpublishing.com
bkroystonpublishing@gmail.com

© Copyright – 2016

All Rights Reserved. No part of this book may be reproduced, stored in a retrieval system, or transmitted by any means without the written permission of the author.

Cover DESIGNER: TED DONES
TLD GRAPHIC DESIGN
417.396.8295 | P.O.BOX 43881
LOUISVILLE, KY 40243
WWW.MESSENGERSOFFIRE.ORG

ISBN-13: 978-0692666128
ISBN-10: 0692666125
LCCN: 2016935772

All Scriptures are taken from the KING JAMES VERSION (KJV): public domain or from the version of the bible listed and within the permission for use guidelines.

Printed in the United States of America

From the Author

This book is written for every born again believer that you might truly know what has been made available to you by the Father to defeat the enemies in your life.
Each of these weapons was introduced to me through the Holy Spirit by way of personal study and battle. They have been tested and proven.

As you are introduced and become familiar with each of them and how they work, may you be quick to use them that you may continually walk in **VICTORY!**

Satan is a heavyweight, it's time to alienate, aggravate, devastate, annihilate, and amputate this immigrate.

Let's dismantle these demonic forces that have been assigned to abort God's plan for our lives.

"For the weapons of our warfare are not carnal, but mighty through God to the pulling down of strong holds."
2 Corinthians 10:4

Prayer

Father, in your most holy name Jesus. We petition you on the behalf of every reader of this book, that you would empower us with wisdom, knowledge and understanding of your Word, to defeat the enemy daily. For the weapons of our warfare *are* not carnal, but mighty through God to the pulling down of strong holds according to 2 Corinthians 10:4. We stand united to dismantle the evil forces of darkness that comes to steal, kill and destroy the plan that you have for our lives. We thank you Father that this book will be a great resource tool in the hands of your people to accomplish this Kingdom assignment.

We declare and decree, that many lives shall be changed to do greater exploits in Jesus powerful name. Amen.

Apostle Harold R. Henderson

The Living Word Church

Dallas/Fort Worth, TX

Table of Contents

From the Author
Foreword — Apostle Dones
Foreword — Apostle Henderson
Weapons of the Heart — 9

- Obedience — 10
- Submission — 22
- Humility — 24
- Love — 27
- Forgiveness — 32

Weapons of the Mouth — 47

- The Word — 48
- Prayer — 58
- Tongues — 61
- Intercession — 63
- Name of Jesus — 66
- Blood of Jesus — 67
- Prophesy — 68
- Confession — 69
- Encouragement — 71
- Agreement — 73
- Declare and Decree — 75
- Silence — 76

Weapons of the Mind — 79

- Faith — 80
- Peace — 85
- Joy — 87
- Patience — 89
- Remembrance — 90

	Waiting	91
	Laughter	92
Weapons of the Spirit		95
	Authority	96
	The Anointing	98
	Discernment	100
	Hearing	102
	Wisdom	107
Weapons of the Body		115
	Fasting	116
	Health	118
	Celibacy	121
Weapons of the Assistance		123
	Holy Spirit	124
	Angels	125
Weapons of the Noise		127
	Praise	128
	Worship	131
	Clapping	135
	Shouting	136
	Hallelujah	140
	Thanksgiving	141
Weapons of the Maturity		143
	Vision	144
	Writing	145
	Focus	147
	Determination	150
	Persistence	151
	No	153

Weapons of the Pocketbook 155
    Tithing 156
    Sowing 157
Final Weapon 161
    Rest 162
A List of the Enemy's Weapons 165
About the Author 167

Foreword

There are many truths which, if applied, can be life changing. To know the truth will make you free, and all truth originates with the Word of God. Dr. Ruth M Wilson, in her New Book Fully Equipped, will take you step by step on a journey to see the 49 weapons that God has given us to fight against the enemy.

Through years of proclaiming God's Word and her insight into the Scriptures, Dr. Ruth Wilson, will challenge you and guide you in your walk to understanding God's Mercy and Grace. Read this book and continue to apply the principles contained in it and you will find freedom.

Forever Sealed in His Love,

Dr. Ted Dones
Messengers of Fire Ministries

Foreword

I take great joy in writing this foreword and accede to the request of the author, Dr. Ruth M. Wilson in her book, Fully Equipped. In this book, Dr. Ruth Wilson has supplied the reader with a host of weapons for warfare to ensure that we will have great success in our walk with God.

She has accurately used scriptures and definitions to lay a strong foundation in her teaching. Dr. Ruth is a spiritual intercessor who knows about the weapons of warfare and its usage thereof. In receiving this armor, your life as a true disciple of Christ will be blessed.

Apostle Harold R. Henderson

The Living Word Church

Dallas/Fort Worth, TX

Ephesians 6:10-18
King James Version

[10] Finally, my brethren, be strong in the Lord, and in the power of his might.

[11] Put on the whole armour of God, that ye may be able to stand against the wiles of the devil.

[12] For we wrestle not against flesh and blood, but against principalities, against powers, against the rulers of the darkness of this world, against spiritual wickedness in high places.

[13] Wherefore take unto you the whole armour of God, that ye may be able to withstand in the evil day, and having done all, to stand.

[14] Stand therefore, having your loins girt about with truth, and having on the breastplate of righteousness;

[15] And your feet shod with the preparation of the gospel of peace;

[16] Above all, taking the shield of faith, wherewith ye shall be able to quench all the fiery darts of the wicked.

[17] And take the helmet of salvation, and the sword of the Spirit, which is the word of God:

[18] Praying always with all prayer and supplication in the Spirit, and watching thereunto with all perseverance and supplication for all saints;

The Living Bible Version (TLB)

[10] Last of all I want to remind you that your strength must come from the Lord's mighty power within you. [11] Put on all of God's armor so that you will be able to stand safe against all strategies and tricks of Satan. [12] For we are not fighting against people made of flesh and blood, but against persons without bodies—the evil rulers of the unseen world, those mighty satanic beings and great evil princes of darkness who rule this world; and against huge numbers of wicked spirits in the spirit world.

[13] So use every piece of God's armor to resist the enemy whenever he attacks, and when it is all over, you will still be standing up.

[14] But to do this, you will need the strong belt of truth and the breastplate of God's approval. [15] Wear shoes that are able to speed you on as you preach the Good News of peace with God. [16] In every battle you will need faith as your shield to stop the fiery arrows aimed at you by Satan. [17] And you will need the helmet of salvation and the sword of the Spirit—which is the Word of God.

[18] Pray all the time. Ask God for anything in line with the Holy Spirit's wishes. Plead with him, reminding him of your needs, and keep praying earnestly for all Christians everywhere.

The Message Version

¹⁰⁻¹² And that about wraps it up. God is strong, and he wants you strong. So take everything the Master has set out for you, well-made weapons of the best materials. And put them to use so you will be able to stand up to everything the Devil throws your way. This is no afternoon athletic contest that we'll walk away from and forget about in a couple of hours. This is for keeps, a life-or-death fight to the finish against the Devil and all his angels.

¹³⁻¹⁸ Be prepared. You're up against far more than you can handle on your own. Take all the help you can get, every weapon God has issued, so that when it's all over but the shouting you'll still be on your feet. Truth, righteousness, peace, faith, and salvation are more than words. Learn how to apply them. You'll need them throughout your life. God's Word is an indispensable weapon. In the same way, prayer is essential in this ongoing warfare. Pray hard and long. Pray for your brothers and sisters. Keep your eyes open. Keep each other's spirits up so that no one falls behind or drops out.

The body of Christ is engaged in a spiritual battle, and it has intensified over the years because we are closer to the Lord's return. Satan more than ever wants us to doubt God, His Word, our power, dominion and authority, over him, but as the Word says, "The devil is a **LIAR** and there is no truth in him." John 8:44

Our Father has given us spiritual weapons that we may be able to stand against the devil and his army without being knocked down, knocked out, defeated and tempted beyond our ability to resist.

WEAPONS, SOMETHING USED TO INJURE, DEFEAT, OR DESTROY.
AND A MEANS OF CONTENDING AGAINST ANOTHER.

TACTICS, THE SCIENCE OF MANEUVERING FORCES IN COMBAT. THE SKILL OF USING AVAILABLE MEANS TO ACCOMPLISH AN END.

EPHESIANS 6:13 says, Wherefore take unto you the whole armour of God, that ye may be able to withstand in the evil day, and having done all, to stand.

Evil day (periodic demonic onslaughts and satanic assaults)

Having done all (Dressing oneself in God's armor and resisting satan)

GOD'S DEFENSIVE ARMOR AND OUR OFFENSIVE WEAPONS ARE TWO TOTALLY DIFFERENT THINGS. GOD'S ARMOR CONSISTS OF SIX PIECES.

1) **TRUTH** is knowledge of the truth of God's word. The ancient soldier loins (waist) were girt about with a leather belt which held most of the other pieces of his armor. Similarly, the other pieces of our armor depend on, and are held in place by our spiritual belt, our knowledge of the truth of the scripture.
2) **THE BREASTPLATE OF RIGHTEOUSNESS**, (the breastplate which is righteousness) represents a holy character and good moral conduct. Obedience to God's Word produces a godly life (Righteousness)
3) **PREPERATION OF THE GOSPEL OF PEACE**, Eagerness Just as the Roman soldier wore special shoes called caligae on his feet, we must possess a sense of eagerness to advance against the devil and take the fight to him. Such eagerness to contend with Satan comes from the gospel of peace. The gospel gives peace to the believer freeing him

from anxiety though he advances against such a powerful opponent.
4) **THE SHIELD OF FAITH**, taking God at his Word, by believing his promises, never doubting; knowing that such trust will protect us from the enemy's weapons of doubts and fear.
5) **THE HELMET OF SALVATION**, "The hope of Salvation" as described in1 Thessalonians 5:8. "But let us, who are of the day, be sober, putting on the breastplate of faith and love; and for a helmet, the hope of salvation."
6) **SWORD OF THE SPIRIT**, is scripture, the Word of God

Weapons of the Heart

Weapon One

OBEDIENCE is to hear God's Word and conduct one's self accordingly.
The word translated "obey" in the Old Testament means "to hear"

Obedience springs from gratitude for grace received.

1 Samuel 15:22b
Behold, to obey is better than sacrifice, and to hearken than the fat of rams.

The Message Version
He wants you to listen to him! Plain listening is the thing, not staging a lavish religious production.

Next is a list of what obedience does for us:

Our obedience lengthens our days according to 1 Kings 3:14

And if thou wilt walk in my ways, to keep my statutes and my commandments, as thy father David did walk, then I will lengthen thy days.

It keeps the enemy from touching us according to Proverbs 16:7

When a man's ways please the LORD, he maketh even his enemies to be at peace with him.

It is the price of success according to Joshua 1:8

This book of the law shall not depart out of thy mouth; but thou shalt meditate therein day and night, that thou **mayest observe to do according to all that is written therein: for then thou shalt make thy way prosperous, and then thou shalt have good success.**

It is the key to being abundantly blessed according to Deuteronomy 28:1-13

And it shall come to pass, if thou shalt hearken diligently unto the voice of the LORD thy God, to observe and to do all his commandments which I command thee this day, that the LORD thy God will set thee on high above all nations of the earth:

2 And all these blessings shall come on thee, and overtake thee, if thou shalt hearken unto the voice of the LORD thy God.

3 Blessed shalt thou be in the city, and blessed shalt thou be in the field.

4 Blessed shall be the fruit of thy body, and the fruit of thy ground, and the fruit of thy cattle, the increase of thy kind, and the flocks of thy sheep.

⁵ Blessed shall be thy basket and thy store.

⁶ Blessed shalt thou be when thou comest in, and blessed shalt thou be when thou goest out.

⁷ The LORD shall cause thine enemies that rise up against thee to be smitten before thy face: they shall come out against thee one way, and flee before thee seven ways.

⁸ The LORD shall command the blessing upon thee in thy storehouses, and in all that thou settest thine hand unto; and he shall bless thee in the land which the LORD thy God giveth thee.

⁹ The LORD shall establish thee an holy people unto himself, as he hath sworn unto thee, if thou shalt keep the commandments of the LORD thy God, and walk in his ways.

¹⁰ And all people of the earth shall see that thou art called by the name of the LORD; and they shall be afraid of thee.

¹¹ And the LORD shall make thee plenteous in goods, in the fruit of thy body, and in the fruit of thy cattle, and in the fruit of thy ground, in the land which the LORD sware unto thy fathers to give thee.

¹² The LORD shall open unto thee his good treasure, the heaven to give the rain unto thy land in his season, and to bless all the work of thine hand: and thou shalt lend unto many nations, and thou shalt not borrow.

¹³ And the L ord shall make thee the head, and not the tail; and thou shalt be above only, and thou shalt not be beneath; if that thou hearken unto the commandments of the L ord thy God, which I command thee this day, to observe and to do them:

Obedience is the most powerful weapon of all the weapons; it automatically keeps the enemy at bay/away, except when God permits/allows him to try/test/tempt you. If that be the case then please know and rest in the fact that you are being set up by God for increase in every area of your life.

The saying "He will bless you double for your trouble" is more than just cliché it is the truth and can be proven in the story of Job.

Job's obedience was notice, blessed, and recorded by God.

Job 1:1, 6-10

¹There was a man in the land of Uz, whose name was Job; and that man was perfect and upright, and one that feared God, and eschewed evil.

⁶Now there was a day when the sons of God came to present themselves before the LORD, and Satan came also among them.

⁷And the LORD said unto Satan, Whence comest thou? Then Satan answered the LORD, and said, from going to and fro in the earth, and from walking up and down in it.

⁸And the LORD said unto Satan, Hast thou considered my servant Job, that there is none like him in the earth, a perfect and an upright man, one that feareth God, and escheweth evil?

Contemporary English Version - verse 8

He was a truly good person, who respected God and refused to do evil.

The Message Version- verse 8

He was honest inside and out, a man of his word, who was totally devoted to God and hated evil with a passion

⁹Then Satan answered the LORD, and said, Doth Job fear God for nought?

¹⁰Hast not thou made an hedge about him, and about his house, and about all that he hath on every side? thou hast blessed the work of his hands, and his substance is increased in the land.

Verse 10 Contemporary English Version

"You are like a wall protecting not only him, but his entire family and all his property. You make him successful in whatever he does, and his flocks and herds are everywhere.

Can you feel the anger and hatred coming from Satan?

Satan doesn't feel this way too often, due to the fact that not many of us are standing in the place where Job stood.
Again the Word says Job was "perfect and upright, and one that feared God, and eschewed evil."

Being honest with ourselves, how many of us are really a threat to Satan and his kingdom. Are we truly standing in the place where Job stood? Are we perfect, upright, fearing God, and eschewing evil?
Only you can answer that question.

Perfect, is to be complete; fully informed; completely skilled; perfect in discipline, and complete in moral excellencies.

Be ye therefore perfect, even as your Father who is in heaven is perfect. Matthew 5:48

Job exercised his weapon of obedience daily, which built the hedge that surrounded him and all that was dear to him.

Job's obedience was his I love you and am in love with you to the Father. It was his total trust in the Father that caused him to follow daily instruction, which guaranteed him the victory in all circumstances.

Job gave God his best; he was consistent and persistent in his communion with God. That is why I believe he could sit quiet for seven days, and worship instead of complaining and blaming God.

This is confirmed in verse 20 of chapter 1
"Then Job arose, and rent his mantle, and shaved his head, and fell down upon the ground, and worshipped,"

Worship would not have been the choice for most of us. Instead we would have used the enemy's weapon against our self which are murmuring and complaining.

We would have cried and called anybody or everybody looking for sympathy, etc. but instead Job worshipped.

Again remember when walking in the spirit of true obedience we are protected, untouchable, and off limits to Satan, unless God opens the door and permits, which again we know that it will be a set up for increase, for us to be blessed tremendously.

As the story goes on, Satan is permitted to afflict Job, and he does it by taking away everything God gave him including his children.

Chapter 1:12-22 LBV

12-13 And the Lord replied to Satan, "You may do anything you like with his wealth, but don't harm him physically."

So Satan went away; and sure enough, not long afterwards when Job's sons and daughters were dining at the oldest brother's house, tragedy struck.

14-15 A messenger rushed to Job's home with this news: "Your oxen were plowing, with the donkeys feeding beside them, when the Sabeans raided us, drove away the animals, and killed all the farmhands except me. I am the only one left."

16 While this messenger was still speaking, another arrived with more bad news: "The fire of God has fallen from heaven and burned up your sheep and all the herdsmen, and I alone have escaped to tell you."

17 Before this man finished, still another messenger rushed in: "Three bands of Chaldeans have driven off your camels and killed your servants, and I alone have escaped to tell you."

[18] As he was still speaking, another arrived to say, "Your sons and daughters were feasting in their oldest brother's home, [19] when suddenly a mighty wind swept in from the desert and engulfed the house so that the roof fell in on them and all are dead; and I alone escaped to tell you."

[20] Then Job stood up and tore his robe in grief[f] and fell down upon the ground before God. [21] "I came naked from my mother's womb," he said, "and I shall have nothing when I die. The Lord gave me everything I had, and they were his to take away. Blessed be the name of the Lord."

[22] In all of this Job did not sin or revile God.

Because Satan was made a liar, and defeated in his attack upon and against Job the first time, he seeks to afflict him a second time, only this time it was physically.

Chapter 2:1-7   LBV

Now the angels came again to present themselves before the Lord, and Satan was with them.

[2] "Where have you come from?" the Lord asked Satan.

"From earth, where I've been watching everything that's going on," Satan replied.

[3] "Well, have you noticed my servant Job?" the Lord asked. "He is the finest man in all the earth—a good

man who fears God and turns away from all evil. And he has kept his faith in me despite the fact that you persuaded me to let you harm him without any cause."

4-5 "Skin for skin," Satan replied. "A man will give anything to save his life. Touch his body with sickness, and he will curse you to your face!"

6 "Do with him as you please," the Lord replied; "only spare his life."

7 So Satan went out from the presence of the Lord and struck Job with a terrible case of boils from head to foot. 8 Then Job took a broken piece of pottery to scrape himself and sat among the ashes.

Again Satan was defeated, Job held onto his integrity

Now desperate to prove his point and be right in his statement to God, Satan comes in with a final blow. His weapon this time was the closet person to Job, his heart, his wife.

9 His wife said to him, "Are you still trying to be godly when God has done all this to you? Curse him and die."

10 But he replied, "You talk like some heathen woman. What? Shall we receive only pleasant things from the hand of God and never anything unpleasant?" So in all this Job said or did nothing wrong.

The weapon of **OBEDIENCE** will keep the enemy away from you and yours. Even your name will be off limits to his lips. Just remember when he is allowed excess, if you didn't leave the door open, God did and you are being set up for a double blessing.

Chapter 42:10-17

¹⁰ And the Lord turned the captivity of Job, when he prayed for his friends: also the Lord gave Job twice as much as he had before.

¹¹ Then came there unto him all his brethren, and all his sisters, and all they that had been of his acquaintance before, and did eat bread with him in his house: and they bemoaned him, and comforted him over all the evil that the Lord had brought upon him: every man also gave him a piece of money, and everyone an earring of gold.

¹² So the Lord blessed the latter end of Job more than his beginning: for he had fourteen thousand sheep, and six thousand camels, and a thousand yoke of oxen, and a thousand she asses.

¹³ He had also seven sons and three daughters.

¹⁴ And he called the name of the first, Jemima; and the name of the second, Kezia; and the name of the third, Kerenhappuch.

[15] And in all the land were no women found so fair as the daughters of Job: and their father gave them inheritance among their brethren.

[16] After this lived Job an hundred and forty years, and saw his sons, and his sons' sons, even four generations. [17] So Job died, being old and full of days.

Weapon Two

Submission the state of being obedient: the act of accepting the authority or control of someone else.

James 4:7
Submit yourselves therefore to God. Resist the devil, and he will flee from you.

First and foremost we are to submit to God, our Father and Creator, second to leadership, pastors, teachers, local authority, etc. third to each other.

Hebrews 13:17
Obey them that have the rule over you, and submit yourselves: for they watch for your souls, as they that must give account, that they may do it with joy, and not with grief: for that is unprofitable for you.

Ephesians 5:21
Submitting yourselves one to another in the fear of God.

Jesus exemplified the ultimate submission in Luke 22:41-42

[41] And he was withdrawn from them about a stone's cast, and kneeled down, and prayed,

[42] Saying, Father, if thou be willing, remove this cup from me: nevertheless not my will, but thine, be done.

We must have no will of our own but that which is the Lord's, to obey Him at all cost, that is submission at its best.

Weapon Three

Humility is freedom from pride and arrogance; a modest estimate of one's own worth.

1 Peter 5:6

Humble yourselves therefore under the mighty hand of God, that he may exalt you in due time:

Luke 14:11
For whosoever exalteth himself shall be abased; and he that humbleth himself shall be exalted.

Proverbs 22:4
By humility and the fear of the Lord are riches, and honour, and life.

2 Chronicles 7:14
If my people, which are called by my name, shall humble themselves, and pray, and seek my face, and turn from their wicked ways; then will I hear from heaven, and will forgive their sin, and will heal their land.

Examples of humility:

Gideon
Judges 6:15
And he said unto him, Oh my Lord, wherewith shall I

save Israel? Behold, my family is poor in Manasseh, and I am the least in my father's house.

King David
1 Samuel 18:18;23
And David said unto Saul, Who am I? and what is my life, or my father's family in Israel, that I should be son in law to the king?

And Saul's servants spake those words in the ears of David.   And David said, Seemeth it to you a light thing to be a king's son in law, seeing that I am a poor man, and lightly esteemed?

King Solomon
1 Kings 3:7
And now, O LORD my God, thou hast made thy servant king instead of David my father: and I am but, little child: I know not how to go out or come in.

What we must understand is that everything we are able to do is because of God. If he removed His spirit from us, where would we be? It is He who wakes us up every morning, walks with us through the day. Gives us gifts and ideas, therefore we have no right to brag but give thanks to him for what He has and is doing in our lives. Without Him we are nothing and without him we can do nothing.

Pride is a weapon of the enemy and will get you knocked and sat down.

Matthew 23:12
And whosoever shall exalt himself shall be abased; and he that shall humble himself shall be exalted.

But those who think themselves great shall be disappointed and humbled; and those who humble themselves shall be exalted. TLB

Weapon Four

LOVE is to be pleased with; to regard with affection.

The first duty of man is to love God. It springs from just views of his attributes or excellencies of character.

Deuteronomy 6:5
And thou shalt love the LORD thy God with all thine heart, and with all thy soul, and with all thy might.

This requires total surrender of the whole being to God. This love for the Father must come from the heart-all inward affections, from the soul-all consciousness, and from the mind-all thoughts.

Second we are instructed to love one another;

John 15:12
This is my commandment, That ye love one another, as I have loved you.

Last but not least we called to love our enemies also.

Matthew 5:44-45a But I say unto you, Love your enemies, bless them that curse you, do good to them that hate you, and pray for them which despitefully use you, and persecute you; [45]That ye may be the children of your Father which is in heaven:

The admonition "Love your enemies" is one of the greatest statements Jesus ever made. This kind of love originates from God himself. We are to love everyone with the love that comes from the Father. This love is proof of our salvation. When we love we leave no opening for hatred, envy, or jealousy. Love causes you to pray when you want to cuss, fight, or kill your enemy.

The Word says, "Dearly beloved, avenge not yourselves, but rather give place unto wrath: for it is written, Vengeance is mine; I will repay, saith the Lord. Therefore if thine enemy hunger, feed him; if he thirst, give him drink: for in so doing thou shalt heap coals of fire on his head. Be not overcome of evil, but overcome evil with good." Romans 12:19-21

Psalm 145:20
The LORD preserveth all them that love him: but all the wicked will he destroy.

Psalm 119:165
Great peace have they which love thy law: and nothing shall offend them.

John 3:16
For God so loved the world, that he gave his only begotten Son, that whosoever believeth in him should not perish, but have everlasting life.

John 13:3-5 Unconditional love of the Son

Jesus knowing that the Father had given all things into his hands, and that he was come from God, and went to God;

[4]He riseth from supper, and laid aside his garments; and took a towel, and girded himself.

[5]After that he poureth water into a bason, and began to wash the disciples' feet, and to wipe them with the towel wherewith he was girded.

Real love will allow you to love your enemy or those close to you that betray you, as Jesus did concerning Judas.

It will cause you to look beyond their faults and ways, and bless them in spite of themselves.

Ephesians 5:2
And walk in love, as Christ also hath loved us, and hath given himself for us an offering and a sacrifice to God for a sweet smelling savour.

The Message Version

¹⁻²Watch what God does, and then you do it, like children who learn proper behavior from their parents. Mostly what God does is love you. Keep company with him and learn a life of love. Observe how Christ loved us. His love was not cautious but extravagant. He didn't love in order to get something from us but to give everything of himself to us. Love like that.

Colossians 3:14
And above all these things put on charity, which is the bond of perfectness.

Contemporary English Version
Love is more important than anything else. It is what ties everything completely together.

1 John 4:16
And we have known and believed the love that God hath to us. God is love; and he that dwelleth in love dwelleth in God, and God in him.

There are three different types of love that I am familiar with and they are, Agape, the highest of the three types of love in the Bible. Jesus Christ showed this kind of divine love to his Father and to all humanity.
Philia, is the type of love in the Bible that we are to practice toward each other. Eros is the

physical, sensual love between a husband and wife.

We must love everybody, regardless if they love us or not, regardless if they do us wrong or not. It's easy to hate, but it's also easy to love. Jesus did!

Weapon Five

FORGIVENESS

Forgive, pardon, to stop feeling anger toward someone who has done something wrong: to stop blaming someone; to give up resentment

Genesis 37 Joseph CEV

³Jacob loved Joseph more than he did any of his other sons, because Joseph was born after Jacob was very old. Jacob had given Joseph a fancy coat ⁴to show that he was his favorite son, and so Joseph's brothers hated him and would not be friendly to him. ⁵One day, Joseph told his brothers what he had dreamed, and they hated him even more. ⁶Joseph said, "Let me tell you about my dream. ⁷We were out in the field, tying up bundles of wheat. Suddenly my bundle stood up, and your bundles gathered around and bowed down to it."

⁸His brothers asked, "Do you really think you are going to be king and rule over us?" **Now they hated Joseph more than ever because of what he had said about his dream**.

⁹Joseph later had another dream, and he told his brothers, "Listen to what else I dreamed. The sun, the moon, and eleven stars bowed down to me."

¹⁰When he told his father about this dream, his father became angry and said, "What's that supposed to mean? Are your mother and I and your brothers all going to come and bow down in front of you?" ¹¹Joseph's **brothers were jealous of him,** but his father kept wondering about the dream.

Joseph had to forgive the ignorance of his father, in not understanding who he was and what he was sharing with him. Then he had to forgive his brothers not only for their jealousy but for their hatred.

Let's look further:

¹²One day when Joseph's brothers had taken the sheep to a pasture near Shechem, ¹³his father Jacob said to him, "I want you to go to your brothers. They are with the sheep near Shechem."

"Yes, sir," Joseph answered.

¹⁴His father said, "Go and find out how your brothers and the sheep are doing. Then come back and let me know." So he sent him from Hebron Valley.

Joseph was near Shechem ¹⁵and wandering through the fields, when a man asked, "What are you looking for?"

¹⁶Joseph answered, "I'm looking for my brothers who are watching the sheep. Can you tell me where they are?"

¹⁷"They're not here anymore," the man replied. "I overheard them say they were going to Dothan."

Joseph left and found his brothers in Dothan. ¹⁸But before he got there, they saw him coming and made plans to kill him. ¹⁹They said to one another, "Look, here comes the hero of those dreams! ²⁰Let's kill him and throw him into a pit and say that some wild animal ate him. Then we'll see what happens to those dreams."

²¹Reuben heard this and tried to protect Joseph from them. "Let's not kill him," he said. ²²"Don't murder him or even harm him. Just throw him into a dry well out here in the desert." Reuben planned to rescue Joseph later and take him back to his father.

²³**When Joseph came to his brothers, they pulled off his fancy coat** ²⁴**and threw him into a dry well**. ²⁵As Joseph's brothers sat down to eat, they looked up and saw a caravan of Ishmaelites coming from Gilead. Their camels were loaded with all kinds of spices that they were taking to Egypt. ²⁶So Judah said, "What will we gain if we kill our brother and hide his body? ²⁷Let's sell him to the Ishmaelites and not harm him. After all, he is our brother." And the others agreed.

²⁸When the Midianite merchants came by, **Joseph's brothers took him out of the well, and for twenty pieces of silver they sold him to the Ishmaelites who took him to Egypt.** ²⁹When Reuben returned to the well and did not find Joseph there, he tore his clothes in sorrow. ³⁰Then he went

back to his brothers and said, "The boy is gone! What am I going to do?"

Joseph had to forgive them for striping him of his coat of many colors that his father had given him. He had to forgive them for putting him in the well, sitting down and eating like he was not there. Then he had to forgive them for selling him to the Midianite merchants for twenty pieces of silver

[31] Joseph's brothers killed a goat and dipped Joseph's fancy coat in its blood. [32] After this, they took the coat to their father and said, "We found this! Look at it carefully and see if it belongs to your son."

[33] Jacob knew it was Joseph's coat and said, "It's my son's coat! Joseph has been torn to pieces and eaten by some wild animal."

[34] Jacob mourned for Joseph a long time, and to show his sorrow he tore his clothes and wore sackcloth. [35] All of Jacob's children came to comfort him, but he refused to be comforted. "No," he said, "I will go to my grave, mourning for my son." So Jacob kept on grieving. [36] Meanwhile, the Midianites had sold Joseph in Egypt to a man named Potiphar, who was the king's official in charge of the palace guard.

The list is piling up of offenses that Joseph's had to forgive. Forgiveness in the kingdom is not a choice, it is a must.

Now he has to forgive the brothers for separating him from his family.

Genesis 39

Joseph and Potiphar's Wife

¹The Ishmaelites took Joseph to Egypt and sold him to Potiphar, the king's official in charge of the palace guard. ²⁻³So Joseph lived in the home of Potiphar, his Egyptian owner. Soon Potiphar realized that the LORD was helping Joseph to be successful in whatever he did. ⁴Potiphar liked Joseph and made him his personal assistant, putting him in charge of his house and all of his property. ⁵Because of Joseph, the LORD began to bless Potiphar's family and fields. ⁶Potiphar left everything up to Joseph, and with Joseph there, the only decision he had to make was what he wanted to eat.

Joseph was well-built and handsome, ⁷and Potiphar's wife soon noticed him. She asked him to make love to her, ⁸but he refused and said, "My master isn't worried about anything in his house, because he has placed me in charge of everything he owns. ⁹No one in my master's house is more important than I am. The only thing he hasn't given me is you, and that's because you are his wife. I won't sin against God by doing such a terrible thing as this." ¹⁰She kept begging Joseph day after day, but he refused to do what she wanted or even to go near her.

¹¹One day, Joseph went to Potiphar's house to do his work, and none of the other servants were there. ¹²Potiphar's wife grabbed hold of his coat and said,

"Make love to me!" Joseph ran out of the house, leaving her hanging onto his coat.

[13]When this happened, [14]she called in her servants and said, "Look! This Hebrew has come just to make fools of us. He tried to rape me, but I screamed for help. [15]And when he heard me scream, he ran out of the house, leaving his coat with me."

[16]Potiphar's wife kept Joseph's coat until her husband came home. [17]Then she said, "That Hebrew slave of yours tried to rape me! [18]But when I screamed for help, he left his coat and ran out of the house."

[19]Potiphar became very angry [20]and threw Joseph in the same prison where the king's prisoners were kept.

While Joseph was in prison, [21]the LORD helped him and was good to him. He even made the jailer like Joseph so much that [22]he put him in charge of the other prisoners and of everything that was done in the jail. [23]The jailer did not worry about anything, because the LORD was with Joseph and made him successful in all that he did.

Joseph was 17 years old when he was sold into slavery (Genesis 37:2). He was 30 when Pharaoh promoted him (Genesis 41:46), and had been in prison for two years before that (Genesis 41:1). Therefore he was in Potiphar's house for 11 years and she was after him for at least 10 years of that time.

In prison, now Joseph not only had to forgive his brothers and their offenses, he now has to forgive Mr. and Mrs. Potiphar. One would say, that this is a little bit much, but think about all the people that have done you wrong over the years.

Genesis 40

Joseph Tells the Meaning of the Prisoners' Dreams

1-3 While Joseph was in prison, both the king's personal servant and his chief cook made the king angry. So he had them thrown into the same prison with Joseph. **4** They spent a long time in prison, and Potiphar, the official in charge of the palace guard, made Joseph their servant. **5** One night each of the two men had a dream, but their dreams had different meanings. **6** The next morning, when Joseph went to see the men, he could tell they were upset, **7** and he asked, "Why are you so worried today?"

8 "We each had a dream last night," they answered, "and there is no one to tell us what they mean."

Joseph replied, "Doesn't God know the meaning of dreams? Now tell me what you dreamed."

9 The king's personal servant told Joseph, "In my dream I saw a vine **10** with three branches. As soon as it budded, it blossomed, and its grapes became ripe. **11** I held the king's cup and squeezed the grapes into it, and then I gave the cup to the king."

¹²Joseph said: This is the meaning of your dream. The three branches stand for three days, ¹³and in three days the king will pardon you. He will make you his personal servant again, and you will serve him his wine, just as you used to do. ¹⁴But when these good things happen, please don't forget to tell the king about me, so I can get out of this place. ¹⁵I was kidnapped from the land of the Hebrews, and here in Egypt I haven't done anything to deserve being thrown in jail.

¹⁶When the chief cook saw that Joseph had given a good meaning to the dream, he told Joseph, "I also had a dream. In it I was carrying three breadbaskets stacked on top of my head. ¹⁷The top basket was full of all kinds of baked things for the king, but birds were eating them."

¹⁸Joseph said:

This is the meaning of your dream. The three baskets are three days, ¹⁹and in three days the king will cut off your head. He will hang your body on a pole, and birds will come and peck at it.

²⁰Three days later, while the king was celebrating his birthday with a dinner for his officials, he sent for his personal servant and the chief cook. ²¹He put the personal servant back in his old job ²²and had the cook put to death.

Everything happened just as Joseph had said it would, ²³but the king's personal servant completely forgot about Joseph.

Again another offence to be forgiven, people makes promises that they don't keep, which will cause you to operate in the spirit of offence, which again is one of Satan's weapons.

Now at God's appointed time:

Genesis 41

Joseph Interprets the King's Dreams
[1]Two years later the king of Egypt dreamed he was standing beside the Nile River. [2]Suddenly, seven fat, healthy cows came up from the river and started eating grass along the bank. [3]Then seven ugly, skinny cows came up out of the river and [4]ate the fat, healthy cows. When this happened, the king woke up. [5]The king went back to sleep and had another dream. This time seven full heads of grain were growing on a single stalk. [6]Later, seven other heads of grain appeared, but they were thin and scorched by the east wind. [7]The thin heads of grain swallowed the seven full heads. Again the king woke up, and it had only been a dream.

[8]The next morning the king was upset. So he called in his magicians and wise men and told them what he had dreamed. None of them could tell him what the dreams meant.

[9]The king's personal servant said:

Now I remember what I was supposed to do. **10**When you were angry with me and your chief cook, you threw us both in jail in the house of the captain of the guard. **11**One night we both had dreams, and each dream had a different meaning. **12**A young Hebrew, who was a servant of the captain of the guard, was there with us at the time. When we told him our dreams, he explained what each of them meant, **13**and everything happened just as he said it would. I got my job back, and the cook was put to death.

14The king sent for Joseph, who was quickly brought out of jail. He shaved, changed his clothes, and went to the king.

15The king said to him, "I had a dream, yet no one can explain what it means. I am told that you can interpret dreams."

16 "Your Majesty," Joseph answered, "I can't do it myself, but God can give a good meaning to your dreams."

17The king told Joseph:

I dreamed I was standing on the bank of the Nile River. **18**I saw seven fat, healthy cows come up out of the river, and they began feeding on the grass. **19**Next, seven skinny, bony cows came up out of the river. I have never seen such terrible looking cows anywhere in Egypt. **20**The skinny cows ate the fat ones. **21**But you couldn't tell it, because these skinny cows were just as skinny as they were before. Right away, I woke up.

22I also dreamed that I saw seven heads of grain growing on one stalk. The heads were full and ripe. **23**Then seven other heads of grain came up. They were thin and scorched by a wind from the desert. **24**These heads of grain swallowed the full ones. I told my dreams to the magicians, but none of them could tell me the meaning of the dreams.

25Joseph replied:

Your Majesty, both of your dreams mean the same thing, and in them God has shown what he is going to do. **26**The seven good cows stand for seven years, and so do the seven good heads of grain. **27**The seven skinny, ugly cows that came up later also stand for seven years, as do the seven bad heads of grain that were scorched by the east wind. The dreams mean there will be seven years when there won't be enough grain.

28It is just as I said--God has shown what he intends to do. **29**For seven years Egypt will have more than enough grain, **30**but that will be followed by seven years when there won't be enough. The good years of plenty will be forgotten, and everywhere in Egypt people will be starving. **31**The famine will be so bad that no one will remember that once there had been plenty. **32**God has given you two dreams to let you know that he has definitely decided to do this and that he will do it soon.

33Your Majesty, you should find someone who is wise and will know what to do, so that you can put him in charge of all Egypt. **34**Then appoint some other officials to collect one-fifth of every crop harvested in Egypt during the seven years when there is plenty. **35**Give them the power to collect the grain during those good years and to store it in your cities. **36**It can be stored until it is needed during the seven years when there won't be enough grain in Egypt. This will keep the country from being destroyed because of the lack of food.

Fulfillment of the dream/promise:

Joseph Is Made Governor over Egypt

37The king and his officials liked this plan. **38**So the king said to them, "No one could possibly handle this better than Joseph, since the Spirit of God is with him." **39**The king told Joseph, "God is the one who has shown you these things. No one else is as wise as you are or knows as much as you do. **40**I'm putting you in charge of my palace, and everybody will have to obey you. No one will be over you except me. **41**You are now governor of all Egypt!"

42Then the king took off his royal ring and put it on Joseph's finger. He gave him fine clothes to wear and placed a gold chain around his neck. **43**He also let him ride in the chariot next to his own, and people shouted, "Make way for Joseph!" So Joseph was governor of Egypt.

44The king told Joseph, "Although I'm king, no one in Egypt is to do anything without your permission."

45He gave Joseph the Egyptian name Zaphenath Paneah. And he let him marry Asenath, the daughter of Potiphera, a priest in the city of Heliopolis. Joseph traveled all over Egypt. **46**Joseph was thirty when the king made him governor, and he went everywhere for the king. **47**For seven years there were big harvests of grain. **48**Joseph collected and stored up the extra grain in the cities of Egypt near the fields where it was harvested. **49**In fact, there was so much grain that they stopped keeping record, because it was like counting the grains of sand along the beach.

50Joseph and his wife had two sons before the famine began. **51**Their first son was named Manasseh, which means, "God has let me forget all my troubles and my family back home." **52**His second son was named Ephraim, which means "God has made me a success in the land where I suffered." **53**Egypt's seven years of plenty came to an end, **54**and the seven years of famine began, just as Joseph had said. There was not enough food in other countries, but all over Egypt there was plenty. **55**When the famine finally struck Egypt, the people asked the king for food, but he said, "Go to Joseph and do what he tells you to do."

56The famine became bad everywhere in Egypt, so Joseph opened the storehouses and sold the grain to the Egyptians. **57**People from all over the world came to Egypt, because the famine was severe in their countries.

If Joseph had not used his weapon of forgiveness, he would have been an angry grudge holder, bound in his own personal prison which would have hindered him from reaching his divine destiny.

Many Christians will miss heaven because of unforgiveness.

Remembering the words of Matthew 6:14-15
For if ye forgive men their trespasses, your heavenly Father will also forgive you:

[15] But if ye forgive not men their trespasses, neither will your Father forgive your trespasses.

Luke 17:4

And if he trespass against thee seven times in a day, and seven times in a day turn again to thee, saying, I repent; thou shalt forgive him.

Ephesians 4:32
And be ye kind one to another, tenderhearted, forgiving one another, even as God for Christ's sake hath forgiven you.

Ask the Father to help you use your weapon of **FORGIVENESS**!

Be at peace with all men don't allow Satan's weapon of offense to keep you in bondage and cause you to miss what God has for. Don't allow it to send you to **HELL**.

Be quick to forgive every person that offends you, that lies on you, that talks about you, that mistreats you, that forgets about you, each and every time. FORGIVE and then FORGET IT! Don't allow Satan to use it as a way to torment you.

You will know when you have truly forgiven because you will not flinch, stress, roll your eyes, say anything negative or have to bring up the past in their presence or in a conversation with anybody else.

You will walk in genuine agape love and be able to pray for them with a sincere heart.

Weapons of the Mouth

Weapon Six

The Word of God scripture, the mind, heart and thoughts of God. His way, direction, promises, and life.

2 Timothy 3:16
All scripture is given by inspiration of God, and is profitable for doctrine, for reproof, for correction, for instruction in righteousness:

The Message Version

Every part of Scripture is God-breathed and useful one way or another—showing us truth, exposing our rebellion, correcting our mistakes, training us to live God's way. Through the Word we are put together and shaped for the tasks/destiny/purpose God created us for.

Matthew 4:4
But he answered and said, It is written, Man shall not live by bread alone, but by every word that proceedeth out of the mouth of God.

The Message Version
Jesus answered by quoting Deuteronomy: "It takes more than bread to stay alive. It takes a steady stream of words from God's mouth."

In this passage we are again reminded of the importance of the Word, we need it like we need the physical/natural food. The Word backed by faith equals power, assurance and victory and it is necessary for our everyday survival.

Psalm 107:20
He sent his word, and healed them, and delivered them from their destructions.

The Word of God shows us who we really are

1 Peter 2:9
But ye are a chosen generation, a royal priesthood, an holy nation, a peculiar people; that ye should shew forth the praises of him who hath called you out of darkness into his marvellous light;

We are just like our Father according to Genesis 1:27 So God created man in his own image, in the image of God created he him; male and female created he them.

Words spoken produce fruit, whether good or bad, in fact Proverbs 18:21 says, Death and life are in the power of the tongue: and they that love it shall eat the fruit thereof.

The Word shows us how we look to God in our mess/sin.

Ezekiel 16:1-34
1The LORD said:

2Ezekiel, son of man, remind the people of Jerusalem of their disgusting sins **3**and tell them that I, the LORD God, am saying:

Jerusalem, you were born in the country where Canaanites lived. Your father was an Amorite, and your mother was a Hittite. **4**When you were born, no one cut you loose from your mother or washed your body. No one rubbed your skin with salt and olive oil,] and wrapped you in warm blankets. **5**Not one person loved you enough to do any of these things, and no one even felt sorry for you. You were despised, thrown into a field, and forgotten. **6**I saw you lying there, rolling around in your own blood, and I couldn't let you die. **7**I took care of you, like someone caring for a tender, young plant. You grew up to be a beautiful young woman with perfect breasts and long hair, but you were still naked.

8When I saw you again, you were old enough to have sex. So I covered your naked body with my own robe. Then I solemnly promised that you would belong to me and that I, the LORD God, would take care of you. **9**I washed the blood off you and rubbed your skin with olive oil. **10**I gave you the finest clothes and the most expensive robes, as well as sandals made from the best leather. **11**I gave you bracelets, a necklace, **12**a ring for your nose, some earrings, and a beautiful crown. **13**Your jewelry was gold and silver, and your clothes were made of only the finest material and embroidered linen. Your bread was baked from fine flour, and you ate honey and olive oil. You were as beautiful as a queen, **14**and everyone on earth knew it. I, the LORD God, had helped you become a lovely young woman. **15**You learned that you were attractive enough to have any man you wanted, so you offered yourself to every passerby. **16**You made shrines for yourself and decorated them with some of your clothes. That's where you took your visitors to have sex with them. These things should never have happened! **17**You made idols out of the gold and silver jewelry I gave you, then you sinned by worshiping those idols. **18**You dressed them in the clothes you got from me, and you offered them the olive oil and incense I gave you. **19**I supplied you with fine flour, olive oil, and honey, but you sacrificed it all as offerings to please those idols. I, the LORD God, watched this happen. **20**But you did something even worse than that--you sacrificed your own children to those idols! **21**You slaughtered my children, so you could offer them as sacrifices. **22**You were so busy sinning and being a prostitute that you refused to think about the days when you were young and were rolling around naked in your own blood.

23Now I, the LORD God, say you are doomed! Not only did you do these evil things, **24**but you also built places on every street corner **25**where you disgraced yourself by having sex with anyone who walked by. And you did that more and more every day! **26**To make me angry, you even offered yourself to Egyptians, who were always ready to sleep with you.

27So I punished you by letting those greedy Philistine enemies take over some of your territory. But even they were offended by your disgusting behavior.

28You couldn't get enough sex, so you chased after Assyrians and slept with them. You still weren't satisfied, **29**so you went after Babylonians. But those merchants could not satisfy you either.

30I, the LORD God, say that you were so disgusting that you would have done anything to get what you wanted. **31**You had sex on every street corner, and when you finished, you refused to accept money. That's worse than being a prostitute! **32**You are nothing but an unfaithful wife who would rather have sex with strangers than with your own husband. **33**Prostitutes accept money for having sex, but you bribe men from everywhere to have sex with you. **34**You're not like other prostitutes. Men don't ask you for sex--you offer to pay them!

The Word of God shows me what I can have/His promises.

Isaiah 1:19
If ye be willing and obedient, ye shall eat the good of the land.

Satan knows the Word and knows that it can be used against him as a weapon. Therefore he loves to test the Word in us.

Genesis 3:1-6

¹Now the serpent was more subtle than any beast of the field which the LORD God had made. And he said unto the woman, Yea, hath God said, Ye shall not eat of every tree of the garden?

²And the woman said unto the serpent, We may eat of the fruit of the trees of the garden:

³But of the fruit of the tree which is in the midst of the garden, God hath said, Ye shall not eat of it, neither shall ye touch it, lest ye die.

⁴And the serpent said unto the woman, Ye shall not surely die:

⁵For God doth know that in the day ye eat thereof, then your eyes shall be opened, and ye shall be as gods, knowing good and evil.

⁶And when the woman saw that the tree was good for food, and that it was pleasant to the eyes, and a tree to be desired to make one wise, she took of the fruit thereof, and did eat, and gave also unto her husband with her; and he did eat.

Eve was without excuse, she knew the Word of instruction that God had given them, yet she allowed Satan to trick her. If we know what the Word says, what God has said to us, we can't afford to debate it with Satan, disbelievers, or ourselves, just do what He/it, the Word says.

Eve's problem was a spirit of curiosity, her desire to know, caused her to debate/wrestle with the truth, which then caused her to doubt that which had been told her by the Father. I now understand the saying "Curiosity killed the cat."

Psalm 119:11
Thy word have I hid in mine heart, that I might not sin against thee.

We must get the Word so deep in our spirit that if we try to go to the left or right it will rise up in us and put us back in place. For a minute visualize two swords in combat, one represents Satan/lies/temptation and the other represents God/You/The Truth, now I ask you who's supposed to win.

Psalm 119:105
Thy word is a lamp unto my feet, and a light unto my path.

Through the Word we are led in the direction God desires for us to go,

Psalm 37:23
The steps of a good man are ordered by the LORD: and he delighteth in his way.

Therefore it leaves no room for us to go astray. Verse 31 says, "The law of his God is in his heart; none of his steps shall slide."

We must read and study it daily, as it says in 2 Timothy 2:15
Study to shew thyself approved unto God, a workman that needeth not to be ashamed, rightly dividing the word of truth.

We must spend time every day in the Word then we will know who He/God is, who we are, who the enemy is, the power we possess, and what is expected of us.

The Holy Spirit, the comforter, the teacher, will give us revelation.

John 14:26
But the Comforter, which is the Holy Ghost, whom the Father will send in my name, he shall teach you all things, and bring all things to your remembrance, whatsoever I have said unto you.) Then apply it to my life on a daily basis.

We need the Word to be effective in ministry:

Matthew 8:16
When the even was come, they brought unto him many that were possessed with devils: and he cast out the spirits with his word, and healed all that were sick:

We must understand that the Word of God is powerful.

Hebrews 4:12
For the word of God is quick, and powerful, and sharper than any two-edged sword, piercing even to the dividing asunder of soul and spirit, and of the joints and marrow, and is a discerner of the thoughts and intents of the heart.

The Message Version
12-13 God means what he says. What he says goes. His powerful Word is sharp as a surgeon's scalpel, cutting through everything, whether doubt or defense, laying us open to listen and obey. Nothing and no one is impervious to God's Word. We can't get away from it—no matter what.

The Word of God heals, delivers, and makes one/sets one free. It strengthens, encourages, inspires, directs, it corrects and it also creates.

Romans 4:17 calleth those things which be not as though they were.

Even the centurion soldier knew about the power of the spoken Word.

Matthew 8:8
The centurion answered and said, Lord, I am not worthy that thou shouldest come under my roof: but speak the word only, and my servant shall be healed.

Therefore be determined to sharpen your sword of the spirit. Become a student of the Word. Be ready for any and every lie /challenge the enemy brings to you.

Weapon Seven

Prayer is a dialogue with God, seeking the wisdom of God, thanking him for blessings bestowed, a solemn request for help. Prayer is the raising of one's mind and heart to God or the requesting of good things from God.
The first prayer in the bible was in Genesis 4:26b then began men to call upon the name of the Lord.

Our instruction to pray
1 Thessalonians 5:17
Pray without ceasing

Ephesians 6:18
Praying always with all prayer and supplication in the Spirit, and watching thereunto with all perseverance and supplication for all saints;

Colossians 4:2
Continue in prayer, and watch in the same with thanksgiving;

Luke 18:1
And he spake a parable unto them to this end, that men ought always to pray, and not to faint.

Philippians 4:6
be careful for nothing; but in everything by prayer

and supplication with thanksgiving let your requests be made known unto God.

Luke 6:12 Jesus our example
and it came to pass in those days, that he went out into a mountain to pray, and continued all night in prayer

What it does

James 5:15-16
And the prayer of faith shall save the sick, and the Lord shall raise him up; and if he have committed sins, they shall be forgiven him.
Confess your faults one to another, and pray one for another, that ye may be healed. The effectual fervent prayer of a righteous man availeth much.

Matthew 18:18-19
"Verily I say unto you, Whatsoever ye shall bind on earth shall be bound in heaven: and whatsoever ye shall loose on earth shall be loosed in heaven."
"Again I say unto you, That if two of you shall agree on earth as touching any thing that they shall ask, it shall be done for them of my Father which is in heaven."

Must have faith when you pray

Matthew 21:22
And all things, whatsoever ye shall ask in prayer, believing, ye shall receive.

That's powerful, to know that whatever I ask in prayer, as long as I believe it, it's going to happen. Why, because I will only ask for what is needed and according to His will.

Weapon Eight

Tongues when a person speaks in a language that is unknown to him. This language is either the language of angels or other earthly languages.

Jude 1:20
But ye, beloved, building up yourselves on your most holy faith, praying in the Holy Ghost,

Romans 8:26
Likewise the Spirit also helpeth our infirmities: for we know not what we should pray for as we ought: but the Spirit itself maketh intercession for us with groanings which cannot be uttered.

1 Corinthians 14:2
For he that speaketh in an unknown tongue speaketh not unto men, but unto God: for no man understandeth him; howbeit in the spirit he speaketh mysteries.

1 Corinthians 14:13
Wherefore let him that speaketh in an unknown tongue pray that he may interpret.

Acts 2:4
And they were all filled with the Holy Ghost, and began to speak with other tongues, as the Spirit gave them utterance.

Acts 19:6
And when Paul had laid his hands upon them, the Holy Ghost came on them; and they spake with tongues, and prophesied.

1 Corinthians 14:14
For if I pray in an unknown tongue, my spirit prayeth, but my understanding is unfruitful.

The religious spirit that is running rampant in the earth would have the body of Christ believing it doesn't take all of that, but it does. There are places you go in the spirit realm when you allow the Holy Ghost to pray through you, that you can't go in the natural. The Word says, we don't know how to pray as we ought. So we've got some help, so let him help.

If you do not have your prayer language, ask the Father he will give it to you. I promise you, you will be glad you did.

Weapon Nine

Intercession to Intercede: To cry out to God on the behalf of others, to pray for someone else with intensity.

Prayers of intercession are to be offered on behalf of other people - your friends, family, co-workers, and so on. Do those around you have needs, concerns, or health problems? Then pray on their behalf.

Galatians 6:2
Bear ye one another's burdens, and so fulfil the law of Christ.

Jesus Intercedes For Us
Hebrews 7:25   Wherefore he is able also to save them to the uttermost that come unto God by him, seeing he ever liveth to make intercession for them.

Contemporary English Version Hebrews 7:25
He is forever able to save the people he leads to God, because he always lives to speak to God for them.

Because of the lack of intercession Jesus came

Isaiah 59:16
And he saw that there was no man, and wondered that there was no intercessor: therefore his arm brought salvation unto him; and his righteousness, it sustained him.

Isaiah 59:16 The Message Version

[15-19]God looked and saw evil looming on the horizon so much evil and no sign of Justice.
He couldn't believe what he saw: not a soul around to correct this awful situation.
So he did it himself, took on the work of Salvation, fueled by his own Righteousness.

Romans 8:26-27:34
[26]Likewise the Spirit also helpeth our infirmities: for we know not what we should pray for as we ought: but the Spirit itself maketh intercession for us with groanings which cannot be uttered.

[27]And he that searcheth the hearts knoweth what is the mind of the Spirit, because he maketh intercession for the saints according to the will of God.

Contemporary English Version

[26] In certain ways we are weak, but the Spirit is here to help us. For example, when we don't know what to pray for, the Spirit prays for us in ways that cannot be put into words. [27] All of our thoughts are known to God. He can understand what is in the mind of the Spirit, as the Spirit prays for God's people.

[34] Who is he that condemneth? It is Christ that died, yea rather, that is risen again, who is even at the right hand of God, who also maketh intercession for us. [34] Who is he that condemneth? It is Christ that died, yea rather, that is risen again, who is even at the right hand of God, who also maketh intercession for us.

[34] Or can anyone condemn them? No indeed! Christ died and was raised to life, and now he is at God's right side, speaking to him for us.

Weapon Ten

Name of Jesus

Philippians 2:9-10
[9] Wherefore God also hath highly exalted him, and given him a name which is above every name: That at the name of Jesus every knee should bow, of things in heaven, and things in earth, and things under the earth;

Mark 16:17
And these signs shall follow them that believe; In my name shall they cast out devils; they shall speak with new tongues;

EXAMPLE: THE SEVENTY

Luke 10:17 The seventy-two returned with joy and said, "Lord, even the demons submit to us in **your name**,"

Use his name when coming against the enemy and always end your prayers by saying, "In Jesus name I pray, amen."

Weapon Eleven

Blood of Jesus

BLOOD OF JESUS the blood of Christ is the price that was paid for our freedom and it frees us and helps us overcome temptations

Revelation 12:11
And they overcame him by the blood of the Lamb, and by the word of their testimony; and they loved not their lives unto the death.

Tell Satan, "The blood of Jesus be against you!" He doesn't like being reminded of the blood that Jesus shed for us. It torments him.

Weapon Twelve

Prophesy to utter predictions; to make declaration of events to come.

1 Thessalonians 5:20
Despise not prophesyings.

Ezekiel 37:3-5
³ And he said unto me, Son of man, can these bones live? And I answered, O Lord GOD, thou knowest.

⁴ Again he said unto me, Prophesy upon these bones, and say unto them, O ye dry bones, hear the word of the LORD.

⁵ Thus saith the Lord GOD unto these bones; Behold, I will cause breath to enter into you, and ye shall live:

We need to prophesy over situations and circumstances in our lives, call those things that be not as though they were. Quit saying it is what it is. No it is because you want prophesy over the situation. In the valley of the dry bones, they were dead and dry until Ezekiel prophesied over and to them.

Weapon Thirteen

Confession an open declaration of something

1 John 1:9
If we confess our sins, he is faithful and just to forgive us our sins and to cleanse us from all unrighteousness.

The Word of God says that all have sinned and come short of the glory of God. It says the Spirit is willing but the flesh is weak. Therefore as we stumble/fall/mess up we must be quick to confess to God knowing he will forgive us and give us another chance. Confession keeps us humble and dependent upon Him.

The other confession, open declaration is to say what I want to happen.

Proverbs 18:21
Death and life are in the power of the tongue, and those who love it will eat its fruits.

Romans 4:17b
and calleth those things which be not as though they were.

We must speak life over every situation in our lives.

Weapon Fourteen

Encouragement something that makes someone more determined, hopeful, or confident: something that makes someone more likely to do something

Ephesians 4:29
Let no corrupt communication proceed out of your mouth, but that which is good to the use of edifying, that it may minister grace unto the hearers.

1 Samuel 30:1-6
And it came to pass, when David and his men were come to Ziklag on the third day, that the Amalekites had invaded the south, and Ziklag, and smitten Ziklag, and burned it with fire;

² And had taken the women captives, that were therein: they slew not any, either great or small, but carried them away, and went on their way.

³ So David and his men came to the city, and, behold, it was burned with fire; and their wives, and their sons, and their daughters, were taken captives.

⁴ Then David and the people that were with him lifted up their voice and wept, until they had no more power to weep.

⁵ And David's two wives were taken captives, Ahinoam the Jezreelitess, and Abigail the wife of Nabal the Carmelite.

⁶ And David was greatly distressed; for the people spake of stoning him, because the soul of all the people was grieved, every man for his sons and for his daughters: but David encouraged himself in the LORD his God.

Sometimes you have to encourage yourself, speak life to yourself, or speak life over a situation, just as David did. Because the spirit of discouragement a weapon of Satan's will come in like a flood upon you to take you out. Use your weapon of the Word, a song, whatever it takes to defeat the enemy of discouragement; stay encouraged.

Weapon Fifteen

Agreement when two or more people believe the same thing

Matthew 18:18-19
"Verily I say unto you, Whatsoever ye shall bind on earth shall be bound in heaven: and whatsoever ye shall loose on earth shall be loosed in heaven."
"Again I say unto you, That if two of you shall **agree** on earth as touching anything that they shall ask, it shall be done for them of my Father which is in heaven."

Numbers 14:6-9
⁶ And Joshua the son of Nun, and Caleb the son of Jephunneh, which were of them that searched the land, rent their clothes:

⁷ And they spake unto all the company of the children of Israel, saying, The land, which we passed through to search it, is an exceeding good land.

⁸ If the LORD delight in us, then he will bring us into this land, and give it us; a land which floweth with milk and honey.

⁹ Only rebel not ye against the LORD, neither fear ye the people of the land; for they are bread for us: their defense is departed from them, and the LORD is with us: fear them not.

When two people are on the same page, walking together, going the same way, with one heart, one mind, one spirit, it makes the journey smoother and more powerful.

Surround yourself with people that see, think, and believe like you.

Weapon Sixteen

Declare and Decree determined judicially; resolved; appointed; established in purpose.

Job 22:28
Thou shalt also decree a thing, and it shall be established unto thee: and the light shall shine upon thy ways.

New American Standard Bible
You will also decree a thing, and it will be established for you; And light will shine on your ways.

1 Kings 17:1
And Elijah the Tishbite, who was of the inhabitants of Gilead, said unto Ahab, As the Lord God of Israel liveth, before whom I stand, there shall not be dew nor rain these years, but according to my word.

Open your mouth and tell the enemy what it is and what it's not going to be, backed by faith and watch things happen, watch situations turn around.

Weapon Seventeen

Silence complete absence of sound, quiet, still, no suggestions, no complaints, no murmuring.

Ecclesiastes 3:7b
a time to keep silence, and a time to speak;

When we are silent we can hear and receive instruction from God. When we are silent we are still and are less apt to get in God's way. Remember God sees things we cannot see and he knows things that we do not know. Learn to be still and quiet.

Isaiah 55:8
For my thoughts are not your thoughts, neither are your ways my ways, saith the LORD.

Psalm 46:10
Be still, and know that I am God: I will be exalted among the heathen, I will be exalted in the earth.

Exodus 14:14
The LORD shall fight for you, and ye shall hold your peace.

In the presence of enemies

Joshua 6:10
And Joshua had commanded the people, saying, Ye shall not shout, nor make any noise with your voice, neither shall any word proceed out of your mouth, until the day I bid you shout; then shall ye shout.

Sometimes being quiet is the best weapon against the enemy. He is not a mind reader so he does not know what we're thinking. It's when we open our mouths out of turn and give him information or make stupid statements that don't line up with the Word of God then we are defeated.

Weapons of the Mind

Weapon Eighteen

Faith believes in that which it cannot see with the natural/physical eye.

Faith is trusting God without any doubt or fear. Faith believes in every documented miracle in the Word of God to be so and to be so for me. Lastly, faith is the denouncement of any limitations on God or myself to accomplish anything I set my mind or hands to.

Our faith is first put into action during our acknowledgement of Jesus being the Son of God when receiving salvation.

Romans 10:9
That if thou shalt confess to use t thy mouth the Lord Jesus, and shalt believe in thine heart that God hath raised him from the dead, thou shalt be saved.

The next thing I want you to know is that we all have faith whether we know it or not according to:

Romans 12:3
For I say, through the grace given unto me, to every man that is among you, not to think of himself more highly than he ought to think; but to think soberly,

according as God hath dealt to every man the measure of faith.

What is the measure of faith?
It is that which God decides to start us out with.

Paul encourages us above every weapon we have, to use the shield of faith.

Ephesians 6:16
Above all, taking the shield of faith, wherewith ye shall be able to quench all the fiery darts of the wicked.

Faith is a shield against the enemy; it causes us to stand tall when he comes against us with his weapons of deception, trickery, lies, etc.

Faith reminds us that the weapon may form but it will not prosper.

Faith will stand and say, "If God be for me who can be against me."

Faith will stand and say, "Greater is he that is in me, than he that is in the world. John 4:4

We Must have faith when we pray

Matthew 21:22
And all things, whatsoever ye shall ask in prayer, believing, ye shall receive.

What faith does

James 5:15-16
And the prayer of faith shall save the sick, and the Lord shall raise him up; and if he have committed sins, they shall be forgiven him. Confess your faults one to another, and pray one for another, that ye may be healed. The effectual fervent prayer of a righteous man availeth much.

Matthew 18:18-19
"Verily I say unto you, Whatsoever ye shall bind on earth shall be bound in heaven: and whatsoever ye shall loose on earth shall be loosed in heaven." "Again I say unto you, That if two of you shall agree on earth as touching any thing that they shall ask, it shall be done for them of my Father which is in heaven."

How do I increase my faith?

Romans 10:17
So then faith cometh by hearing, and hearing by the word of God.

As I study the Word of God daily, as I hear the taught/preached Word in my ear, as God answers prayers, as miracles are performed right before my eyes, my faith is increased. It is the way God wants me to walk.

2 Corinthians 5:7
For we walk by faith, not by sight:

That means that if God said it, if the Word said it, we can believe it, we can trust it. No matter what it looks like, no matter what others say, it is so. We can stand on it, we can do it.

It means that being distracted is not an option

James 1:3
Knowing this, that the trying of your faith worketh patience.

Living Bible Version
for when the way is rough, your patience has a chance to grow.

The Message Version
So don't try to get out of anything prematurely. Let it do its work so you become mature and well-developed, not deficient in any way.

Where there is faith, there is no fear, where there is faith, the impossible becomes possible. Where there is faith, there is determination. Where there is faith there is GOD. Satan is no match for the weapon of faith, faith tears down every lie the enemy can come up with. Faith will stand when it looks like it's all over. Faith commands, declares and decrees things to happen.

Remember it is a must in your spiritual walk, and it pleases the Father according to Hebrews 11:6 that says,
But without faith it is impossible to please him: for he that cometh to God must believe that he is, and that he is a rewarder of them that diligently seek him.

Weapon Nineteen

Peace is a state of quiet or tranquility; freedom from disturbance or agitation;

Job 22:21
Acquaint now thyself with him, and be at peace: thereby good shall come unto thee.

Psalm 119:165
Great peace have they which love thy law: and nothing shall offend them.

Isaiah 26:3
Thou wilt keep him in perfect peace, whose mind is stayed on thee: because he trusteth in thee.

1 Peter 5:7
Casting all your care upon him; for he careth for you.

Matthew 6:34
Take therefore no thought for the morrow: for the morrow shall take thought for the things of itself. Sufficient unto the day is the evil thereof.

There is a place in God with and through God that He desires for us to be, it's called perfect peace where we are quick to talk/consult him about everything. Where we don't have to wonder, we'll know. It is a place where we no longer fret, have anxiety attacks, or operate in fear, just peace that surpasses all understanding.

Weapon Twenty

Joy is a feeling of great happiness

Psalm 16:11
Thou wilt shew me the path of life: in thy presence is fulness of joy; at thy right hand there are pleasures for evermore.

Proverbs 15:23
A man hath joy by the answer of his mouth: and a word spoken in due season, how good is it!

John 15:10-11
If ye keep my commandments, ye shall abide in my love; even as I have kept my Father's commandments, and abide in his love.

[11] These things have I spoken unto you, that my joy might remain in you, and that your joy might be full.

James 1:2
My brethren, count it all joy when ye fall into divers temptations;

Contemporary English Version
My brothers and sisters, think of the various tests you encounter as occasions for joy.

There is a place in God that I move beyond just being happy to great happiness which equals joy. It becomes a permanent residence that cannot be disrupted or interrupted. It's my total trust in God to make everything work for my good. Which keeps a smile on my face no matter what.

Weapon Twenty One

Patience is the capacity to endure what is difficult or disagreeable without complaining

Psalm 37:7-9 (Good News Translation)
Be patient and wait for the Lord to act; don't be worried about those who prosper or those who succeed in their evil plans. Don't give in to worry or anger; it only leads to trouble. Those who trust in the Lord will possess the land, but the wicked will be driven out.

Luke 2:25-26   Living Bible Version
That day a man named Simeon, a Jerusalem resident, was in the Temple. He was a good man, very devout, filled with the Holy Spirit and constantly expecting the Messiah to come soon. [26] For the Holy Spirit had revealed to him that he would not die until he had seen him—God's anointed King.

Weapon Twenty Two

Remembrance the retaining or having in mind an idea which had been present before, Power of remembering; limit of time within which a fact can be remembered;

John 14:26
[26] But the Comforter, which is the Holy Ghost, whom the Father will send in my name, he shall teach you all things, and bring all things to your **remembrance,** whatsoever I have said unto you.

The Message Version
[25-27] "I'm telling you these things while I'm still living with you. The Friend, the Holy Spirit whom the Father will send at my request, will make everything plain to you. He will remind you of all the things I have told you.

Sometimes in the midst of what we are going through we forget what God has said, we forget the promises of God, we forget what He's already done and brought us through, but thank God for the Holy Spirit who brings all things to our remembrance.

Weapon Twenty Three

Waiting which means to wait. Wait means to be able to stay in a place patiently and quietly until something happens, until God permits you to move.

Psalm 37:7-9
[7] Rest in the L ORD, and wait patiently for him: fret not thyself because of him who prospereth in his way, because of the man who bringeth wicked devices to pass.

[8] Cease from anger, and forsake wrath: fret not thyself in any wise to do evil.

[9] For evildoers shall be cut off: but those that wait upon the L ORD, they shall inherit the earth.

Isaiah 40:31
But they that wait upon the L ORD shall renew their strength; they shall mount up with wings as eagles; they shall run, and not be weary; and they shall walk, and not faint.

Lamentations 3:25
The Lord is good to those who wait for him, to the soul who seeks him.

If we believe God is in control, if we believe He is a God of timing, if we believe he knows and sees all, we have no need to impatient.

Weapon Twenty Four

Laughter to show that you are happy or that you think something is funny by smiling and making a sound from your throat: to think or say that someone or something is foolish and does not deserve serious attention or respect: to not be bothered by something

Proverbs 17:22
A joyful heart is good medicine, but a crushed spirit dries up the bones.

Psalm 126:2
Then our mouth was filled with laughter, and our tongue with shouts of joy; then they said among the nations, "The Lord has done great things for them."

Job 8:21 He will yet fill your mouth with laughter, and your lips with shouting.

Ecclesiastes 3:4
A time to weep, and a time to laugh; a time to mourn, and a time to dance;

Proverbs 15:13
A glad heart makes a cheerful face, but by sorrow of heart the spirit is crushed.

Psalm 2:4
He who sits in the heavens laughs; the Lord holds them in derision.

Psalm 32:11
Be glad in the Lord, and rejoice, O righteous, and shout for joy, all you upright in heart

Laughter torments the enemy because it is a sign of freedom and total trust in God to make all things work for my good according to Romans 8:28. Besides that it makes one feel better. Remember he wants us depressed, oppressed, isolated, confused, and despondent. Laughter will bring you out of any sad situation.

Weapons of the Spirit

Weapon Twenty Five

Authority is Legal power, or a right to command or to act; as the authority of a prince over subjects,

Genesis 1:26, 28
26 And God said, Let us make man in our image, after our likeness: and let them have dominion over the fish of the sea, and over the fowl of the air, and over the cattle, and over all the earth, and over every creeping thing that creepeth upon the earth.

28 And God blessed them, and God said unto them, Be fruitful, and multiply, and replenish the earth, and subdue it: and have dominion over the fish of the sea, and over the fowl of the air, and over every living thing that moveth upon the earth.

Luke 10:19
Behold, I give unto you power to tread on serpents and scorpions, and over all the power of the enemy: and nothing shall by any means hurt you.

Luke 9:37-43
[37] And it came to pass, that on the next day, when they were come down from the hill, much people met him.

[38] And, behold, a man of the company cried out, saying, Master, I beseech thee, look upon my son: for he is mine only child.

³⁹ And, lo, a spirit taketh him, and he suddenly crieth out; and it teareth him that he foameth again, and bruising him hardly departeth from him.

⁴⁰ And I besought thy disciples to cast him out; and they could not.

⁴¹ And Jesus answering said, O faithless and perverse generation, how long shall I be with you, and suffer you? Bring thy son hither.

⁴² And as he was yet a coming, the devil threw him down, and tare him. And Jesus rebuked the unclean spirit, and healed the child, and delivered him again to his father.

⁴³ And they were all amazed at the mighty power of God.

You have legal authority and power over satan and every demon, now use it.

Weapon Twenty Six

The Anointing is the presence and power of God flowing through, upon, and around one. It gives one, supernatural ability to preach/teach with power, heal the sick, and deliver the tormented. For instance an evangelist is equipped to win the lost, a pastor to lead his flock, and a singer to minister comfort and joy to the listener.

Luke 4:18-19
[18] The Spirit of the Lord is upon me, because he hath anointed me to preach the gospel to the poor; he hath sent me to heal the brokenhearted, to preach deliverance to the captives, and recovering of sight to the blind, to set at liberty them that are bruised, [19] To preach the acceptable year of the Lord..

Isaiah 10:27
And it shall come to pass in that day, that his burden shall be taken away from off thy shoulder, and his yoke from off thy neck, and the yoke shall be destroyed because of the anointing.

Because of the power of God/the anointing upon one in ministering, people can be set free.

Acts 10:36-38

[36] The word which God sent unto the children of Israel, preaching peace by Jesus Christ:

[37] That word, I say, ye know, which was published throughout all Judaea, and began from Galilee, after the baptism which John preached;

[38] How God anointed Jesus of Nazareth with the Holy Ghost and with power: who went about doing good, and healing all that were oppressed of the devil; for God was with him.

Acts 5:15
Insomuch that they brought forth the sick into the streets, and laid them on beds and couches, that at the least the shadow of Peter passing by might overshadow some of them.

Acts 19:12
So that from his body were brought unto the sick handkerchiefs or aprons, and the diseases departed from them, and the evil spirits went out of them.

Weapon Twenty Seven

Discernment brings forth the knowledge of what kind of spirit is motivating a person's thoughts, attitudes, words or actions. It also can reveal the predominant stronghold of Satan in a particular area, so that intercessors and prayer warriors can deal with it. It is a useful gift also when casting out demons.

1 John 4:1
Beloved, believe not every spirit, but try the spirits whether they are of God: because many false prophets are gone out into the world.

Hebrews 5:14
But strong meat belongeth to them that are of full age, even those who by reason of use have their senses exercised to discern both good and evil.

1 Kings 3:9
Give therefore thy servant an understanding heart to judge thy people, that I may discern between good and bad: for who is able to judge this thy so great a people?

Discernment is a gift from God, to be able to see, hear and know beyond what's being said and done.

Acts 5:1-10 (King James Version)

But a certain man named Ananias, with Sapphira his wife, sold a possession, 2 And kept back part of the price, his wife also being privy to it, and brought a certain part, and laid it at the apostles' feet. But Peter said, Ananias, why hath Satan filled thine heart to lie to the Holy Ghost, and to keep back part of the price of the land? 4 Whiles it remained, was it not thine own? and after it was sold, was it not in thine own power? why hast thou conceived this thing in thine heart? thou hast not lied unto men, but unto God. 5 And Ananias hearing these words fell down, and gave up the ghost: and great fear came on all them that heard these things. 6 And the young men arose, wound him up, and carried him out, and buried him. 7 And it was about the space of three hours after, when his wife, not knowing what was done, came in. 8 And Peter answered unto her, Tell me whether ye sold the land for so much? And she said, Yea, for so much. 9 Then Peter said unto her, How is it that ye have agreed together to tempt the Spirit of the Lord? behold, the feet of them which have buried thy husband are at the door, and shall carry thee out. 10 Then fell she down straightway at his feet, and yielded up the ghost: and the young men came in, and found her dead, and, carrying her forth, buried her by her husband.

Weapon Twenty Eight

Hearing to perceive by the ear, listening to; attending to; obeying; observing what is commanded.

Romans 10:17
So then faith cometh by hearing, and hearing by the word of God.

Luke 11:28
But he said, Yea rather, blessed are they that hear the word of God, and keep it.

John 8:47
He that is of God heareth God's words: ye therefore hear them not, because ye are not of God.

John 10:27
My sheep hear my voice, and I know them, and they follow me:

Isaiah 30:21
And thine ears shall hear a word behind thee, saying, This is the way, walk ye in it, when ye turn to the right hand, and when ye turn to the left.

1 Samuel 3:1-15
And the child Samuel ministered unto the Lord before

Eli. And the word of the Lord was precious in those days; there was no open vision.

² And it came to pass at that time, when Eli was laid down in his place, and his eyes began to wax dim, that he could not see;

³ And ere the lamp of God went out in the temple of the Lord, where the ark of God was, and Samuel was laid down to sleep;

⁴ That the Lord called Samuel: and he answered, Here am I.

⁵ And he ran unto Eli, and said, Here am I; for thou calledst me. And he said, I called not; lie down again. And he went and lay down.

⁶ And the Lord called yet again, Samuel. And Samuel arose and went to Eli, and said, Here am I; for thou didst call me. And he answered, I called not, my son; lie down again.

⁷ Now Samuel did not yet know the Lord, neither was the word of the Lord yet revealed unto him.

⁸ And the Lord called Samuel again the third time. And he arose and went to Eli, and said, Here am I; for thou didst call me. And Eli perceived that the Lord had called the child.

⁹ Therefore Eli said unto Samuel, Go, lie down: and it shall be, if he call thee, that thou shalt say, Speak, Lord; for thy servant heareth. So Samuel went and lay down in his place.

¹⁰ And the Lord came, and stood, and called as at other times, Samuel, Samuel. Then Samuel answered, Speak; for thy servant heareth.

¹¹ And the Lord said to Samuel, Behold, I will do a thing in Israel, at which both the ears of every one that heareth it shall tingle.

¹² In that day I will perform against Eli all things which I have spoken concerning his house: when I begin, I will also make an end.

¹³ For I have told him that I will judge his house for ever for the iniquity which he knoweth; because his sons made themselves vile, and he restrained them not.

¹⁴ And therefore I have sworn unto the house of Eli, that the iniquity of Eli's house shall not be purged with sacrifice nor offering forever.

¹⁵ And Samuel lay until the morning, and opened the doors of the house of the Lord. And Samuel feared to shew Eli the vision.

1 Kings 17:2-5
² And the word of the Lord came unto him, saying,

³ Get thee hence, and turn thee eastward, and hide thyself by the brook Cherith, that is before Jordan.

⁴ And it shall be, that thou shalt drink of the brook; and I have commanded the ravens to feed thee there.

⁵ So he went and did according unto the word of the LORD: for he went and dwelt by the brook Cherith, that is before Jordan.

2 Chronicles 1:6-12
⁶ And Solomon went up thither to the brasen altar before the LORD, which was at the tabernacle of the congregation, and offered a thousand burnt offerings upon it.

⁷ In that night did God appear unto Solomon, and said unto him, Ask what I shall give thee.

⁸ And Solomon said unto God, Thou hast shewed great mercy unto David my father, and hast made me to reign in his stead.

⁹ Now, O LORD God, let thy promise unto David my father be established: for thou hast made me king over a people like the dust of the earth in multitude.

¹⁰ Give me now wisdom and knowledge, that I may go out and come in before this people: for who can judge this thy people, that is so great?

¹¹ And God said to Solomon, Because this was in thine heart, and thou hast not asked riches, wealth, or honour, nor the life of thine enemies, neither yet hast asked long life; but hast asked wisdom and knowledge for thyself, that thou mayest judge my people, over whom I have made thee king:

¹² Wisdom and knowledge is granted unto thee; and I will give thee riches, and wealth, and honour, such as

none of the kings have had that have been before thee, neither shall there any after thee have the like.

We must be able to hear God in this hour that we might be able to follow his instruction and direction, which will bring forth more victories and less tragedies.

Weapon Twenty Nine

Wisdom The right use or exercise of knowledge; Quickness of intellect; knowledge that is gained by having many experiences in life; the natural ability to understand things that most other people cannot understand

Proverbs 3:13-18
Happy is the man that findeth wisdom, and the man that getteth understanding.

[14] For the merchandise of it is better than the merchandise of silver, and the gain thereof than fine gold.

[15] She is more precious than rubies: and all the things thou canst desire are not to be compared unto her.

[16] Length of days is in her right hand; and in her left hand riches and honour.

[17] Her ways are ways of pleasantness, and all her paths are peace.

[18] She is a tree of life to them that lay hold upon her: and happy is every one that retaineth her.

The Living Bible Version   13-15
The man who knows right from wrong and has good judgment and common sense is happier than the man

who is immensely rich! For such wisdom is far more valuable than precious jewels. Nothing else compares with it. [16-17] Wisdom gives: a long, good life, riches, honor, pleasure, peace. [18] Wisdom is a tree of life to those who eat her fruit; happy is the man who keeps on eating it.

The Message Version   13-18
You're blessed when you meet Lady Wisdom, when you make friends with Madame Insight.
She's worth far more than money in the bank; her friendship is better than a big salary.
Her value exceeds all the trappings of wealth; nothing you could wish for holds a candle to her.
With one hand she gives long life, with the other she confers recognition.
Her manner is beautiful, her life wonderfully complete.
She's the very Tree of Life to those who embrace her. Hold her tight—and be blessed!

James 3:17
But the wisdom that is from above is first pure, then peaceable, gentle, and easy to be intreated, full of mercy and good fruits, without partiality, and without hypocrisy.

Living Bible Version
But the wisdom that comes from heaven is first of all pure and full of quiet gentleness. Then it is peace-loving and courteous. It allows discussion and is willing to yield to others; it is full of mercy and good

deeds. It is wholehearted and straightforward and sincere.

How to receive it:

James 1:5
If any of you lack wisdom, let him ask of God, that giveth to all men liberally, and upbraideth not; and it shall be given him.

Encouraged to have and use wisdom:

Proverbs 19:20
Hear counsel, and receive instruction, that thou mayest be wise in thy latter end.

The Message Version
Take good counsel and accept correction— that's the way to live wisely and well.

Ephesians 5:15-17
See then that ye walk circumspectly, not as fools, but as wise,

[16] Redeeming the time, because the days are evil.

[17] Wherefore be ye not unwise, but understanding what the will of the Lord is.

Living Bible Version
So be careful how you act; these are difficult days. Don't be fools; be wise: make the most of every opportunity you have for doing good. [17] Don't act

thoughtlessly, but try to find out and do whatever the Lord wants you to.

Solomon asked God for wisdom.
1 Kings 3:5-14
In Gibeon the Lord appeared to Solomon in a dream by night: and God said, Ask what I shall give thee.

6 And Solomon said, Thou hast shewed unto thy servant David my father great mercy, according as he walked before thee in truth, and in righteousness, and in uprightness of heart with thee; and thou hast kept for him this great kindness, that thou hast given him a son to sit on his throne, as it is this day.

7 And now, O Lord my God, thou hast made thy servant king instead of David my father: and I am but a little child: I know not how to go out or come in.

8 And thy servant is in the midst of thy people which thou hast chosen, a great people, that cannot be numbered nor counted for multitude.

9 Give therefore thy servant an understanding heart to judge thy people, that I may discern between good and bad: for who is able to judge this thy so great a people?

10 And the speech pleased the Lord, that Solomon had asked this thing.

11 And God said unto him, Because thou hast asked this thing, and hast not asked for thyself long life; neither hast asked riches for thyself, nor hast asked

the life of thine enemies; but hast asked for thyself understanding to discern judgment;

¹² Behold, I have done according to thy words: lo, I have given thee a wise and an understanding heart; so that there was none like thee before thee, neither after thee shall any arise like unto thee.

¹³ And I have also given thee that which thou hast not asked, both riches, and honour: so that there shall not be any among the kings like unto thee all thy days.

¹⁴ And if thou wilt walk in my ways, to keep my statutes and my commandments, as thy father David did walk, then I will lengthen thy days.

We need wisdom in the kingdom and in our everyday lives, that we might make the right choices at the right time; that we might say the right things always and even be silent when we need to. Pray daily for wisdom, this will help you out smart the enemy.

1 Kings 3:16-28
Then came there two women, that were harlots, unto the king, and stood before him.

¹⁷ And the one woman said, O my lord, I and this woman dwell in one house; and I was delivered of a child with her in the house.

[18] And it came to pass the third day after that I was delivered, that this woman was delivered also: and we were together; there was no stranger with us in the house, save we two in the house.

[19] And this woman's child died in the night; because she overlaid it.

[20] And she arose at midnight, and took my son from beside me, while thine handmaid slept, and laid it in her bosom, and laid her dead child in my bosom.

[21] And when I rose in the morning to give my child suck, behold, it was dead: but when I had considered it in the morning, behold, it was not my son, which I did bear.

[22] And the other woman said, Nay; but the living is my son, and the dead is thy son. And this said, No; but the dead is thy son, and the living is my son. Thus they spake before the king.

[23] Then said the king, The one saith, This is my son that liveth, and thy son is the dead: and the other saith, Nay; but thy son is the dead, and my son is the living.

[24] And the king said, Bring me a sword. And they brought a sword before the king.

[25] And the king said, Divide the living child in two, and give half to the one, and half to the other.

[26] Then spake the woman whose the living child was unto the king, for her bowels yearned upon her son,

and she said, O my lord, give her the living child, and in no wise slay it. But the other said, Let it be neither mine nor thine, but divide it.

²⁷ Then the king answered and said, Give her the living child, and in no wise slay it: she is the mother thereof.

²⁸ And all Israel heard of the judgment which the king had judged; and they feared the king: for they saw that the wisdom of God was in him, to do judgment.

Weapons of the Body

Weapon Thirty

Fasting is voluntary abstinence from food, denying the flesh of the physical food for the spiritual food. The award is a closer walk with the Father and revelation, hidden mysteries revealed.

Fasting takes one to other levels and dimensions in God/in the kingdom. You can hear God clearer, revelation comes easier. You are empowered, encouraged, and strengthened through fasting.
It is also the best way for a child of God to be disciplined and humbled.

There are times when God will call us to a personal fast himself through your spirit or He will instruct your Pastor to call a corporate fast for the whole body/ministry.

Isaiah 58:6-7
Is not this the fast that I have chosen? to loose the bands of wickedness, to undo the heavy burdens, and to let the oppressed go free, and that ye break every yoke?

Jesus told his disciples that some things will only happen after you have been fasting.

Matthew 17:21
Howbeit this kind goeth not out but by prayer and fasting.

There are different types of fasts. There is the Daniel fast and that is vegetables and water only. There is another Daniel fast that is fruits, vegetables and water only. Then there is the water only fast. Then there is the water and juice fast. Then there are some people that fast and eat only one meal a day. There are length of days for fasting and they can be 3, 7, 21 or 40 days. Last but not least, pray much, stay in your word and don't overly exert yourself when fasting.

Weapon Thirty One

Health the condition of being well or free from disease: the overall condition of someone's body or mind

3 John 1:2
Beloved, I wish above all things that thou mayest prosper and be in health, even as thy soul prospereth.

Amplified Version
Beloved, I pray that in every way you may succeed *and* prosper and be in good health [physically], just as [I know] your soul prospers [spiritually].

Common English Bible
Dear friend, I'm praying that all is well with you and that you enjoy good health in the same way that you prosper spiritually.

1 Corinthians 3:17
If any man defile the temple of God, him shall God destroy; for the temple of God is holy, which temple ye are.

The Message Version
16-17 You realize, don't you, that you are the temple of God, and God himself is present in you? No one will get by with vandalizing God's temple, you can be sure

of that. God's temple is sacred—and you, remember, *are* the temple.

1 Corinthians 10:31
Whether therefore ye eat, or drink, or whatsoever ye do, do all to the glory of God.

Isaiah 53:4-5
[4] Surely he hath borne our griefs, and carried our sorrows: yet we did esteem him stricken, smitten of God, and afflicted.

[5] But he was wounded for our transgressions, he was bruised for our iniquities: the chastisement of our peace was upon him; and with his stripes we are healed.

The Living Bible Version
Yet it was *our* grief he bore, *our* sorrows that weighed him down. And we thought his troubles were a punishment from God, for his *own* sins! [5] But he was wounded and bruised for *our* sins. He was beaten that we might have peace; he was lashed—and we were healed!

1 Peter 2:24
Who his own self bare our sins in his own body on the tree, that we, being dead to sins, should live unto righteousness: by whose stripes ye were healed.

The Living Bible Version
He personally carried the load of our sins in his own body when he died on the cross so that we can be finished with sin and live a good life from now on. For his wounds have healed ours!

Genesis 1:29
And God said, Behold, I have given you every herb bearing seed, which is upon the face of all the earth, and every tree, in the which is the fruit of a tree yielding seed; to you it shall be for meat.

Psalm 107:20
He sent his word, and healed them, and delivered them from their destructions.

Psalm 103:2-3
Bless the LORD, O my soul, and forget not all his benefits:

[3] Who forgiveth all thine iniquities; who healeth all thy diseases;

My Brothers and Sisters, God wants us healthy, no matter the age. He does not want us over weight with all kinds of diseases, on all kinds of medicines. That's a lie and trick of the enemy, can't enjoy life because of limitations due to sickness. Purpose in your heart this year to live and not die.

Weapon Thirty Two

Celibacy abstention from sexual intercourse

1 Corinthians 6:18-20
[18] Flee fornication. Every sin that a man doeth is without the body; but he that committeth fornication sinneth against his own body.

[19] What? know ye not that your body is the temple of the Holy Ghost which is in you, which ye have of God, and ye are not your own?

[20] For ye are bought with a price: therefore glorify God in your body, and in your spirit, which are God's.

Weapon of the Assistance

Weapon Thirty Three

The Holy Spirit the third part of the Trinity (Father, Son, & Holy Spirit)

John 14:26
But the Comforter, which is the Holy Ghost, whom the Father will send in my name, he shall teach you all things, and bring all things to your remembrance, whatsoever I have said unto you.

John 16:13
Howbeit when he, the Spirit of truth, is come, he will guide you into all truth: for he shall not speak of himself; but whatsoever he shall hear, that shall he speak: and he will shew you things to come.

Acts 1:8K
But ye shall receive power, after that the Holy Ghost is come upon you:

Weapon Thirty Four

Angels a spirit, or a spiritual intelligent being employed by God to communicate his will to man.

Daniel 10:13
But the prince of the kingdom of Persia withstood me one and twenty days: but, lo, **Michael**, one of the chief princes, came to help me; and I remained there with the kings of Persia.

Revelation 12:7
And there was war in heaven: **Michael** and his angels fought against the dragon; and the dragon fought and his angels,

We have angels that are assigned to us, ministering angels, guardian angels, and warring angels. Know that they are there at all times waiting to be put to work on your behalf.

Weapon of the Noise

Weapon Thirty Five

PRAISE

Satan hates to hear us praise God.
It is a familiar sound to him, a constant reminder of who he used to be and what he can never be again. Praise is like blowing a dog whistle at Satan, it hurts his ears.
Praise is our thanks unto God for who He is, for what He has done, and for what we believe Him to do as we walk by faith.
Praise is a weapon that brings confusion upon the enemy

Psalm 149:6-9
Let the high praises of God be in their mouth, and a two-edged sword in their hand; To execute vengeance upon the heathen, and punishments upon the people; To bind their kings with chains, and their nobles with fetters of iron; To execute upon them the judgment written: this honour have all his saints. Praise ye the LORD.

EXAMPLE:
2 Chronicles 20:21-23
And when he had consulted with the people, he appointed singers unto the LORD, and that should praise the beauty of holiness, as they went out before the army, and to say, Praise the LORD; for his mercy endureth for ever.

And when they began to sing and to praise, the LORD set ambushments against the children of Ammon, Moab, and mount Seir, which were come against Judah; and they were smitten.
For the children of Ammon and Moab stood up against the inhabitants of mount Seir, utterly to slay and destroy them: and when they had made an end of the inhabitants of Seir, every one helped to destroy another."

We are encouraged to praise him always

Hebrews 13:15
By him therefore let us offer the sacrifice of praise to God continually, that is, the fruit of our lips giving thanks to his name.

The psalmist made a commitment to praise God daily, what is your commitment.

Psalm 119:164
Seven times a day do I praise thee because of thy righteous judgments.

Why should we praise God?

Psalm 147:1
Praise ye the Lord: for it is good to sing praises unto our God; for it is pleasant; and praise is comely.

Too often I've heard people say, "When praises go up blessings come down." That is

not true. If anything we are encouraged and strengthened through our praise. Our blessings come from our obedience and faith in asking according to His will.

Weapon Thirty Six

WORSHIP to perform acts of adoration, paying divine honors to; treating with supreme reverence;
Worship is the continuous sound in heaven's throne room, and when we connect with that worship, we create a holy connection between heaven and earth.

What the Church needs to understand is that our worship puts demonic forces to flight, because they can't stand that type and level of intimacy. In worship we are hidden in the Father, we become one with him.

Job 1:20
Then Job arose, and rent his mantle, and shaved his head, and fell down upon the ground, and worshipped,

Job had an inward excitement he counted It an honor to be afflicted, in fact he was operating in James 1:2-8 which says,

My brethren, count it all joy when ye fall into divers temptations; Knowing this, that the trying of your faith worketh patience. But let patience have her perfect work, that ye may be perfect and entire, wanting nothing.

2 Chronicles 7:3
And when all the children of Israel saw how the fire came down, and the glory of the LORD upon the house, they bowed themselves with their faces to the ground upon the pavement, and worshipped, and praised the LORD, saying, For he is good; for his mercy endureth forever.

True worship can only come out of one, when there is a true desire to be closer to God and when one is truly thankful for what God has already done.

Revelation 4:1-10
After this I looked, and, behold, a door was opened in heaven: and the first voice which I heard was as it were of a trumpet talking with me; which said, Come up hither, and I will shew thee things which must be hereafter.

[2] And immediately I was in the spirit: and, behold, a throne was set in heaven, and one sat on the throne.

[3] And he that sat was to look upon like a jasper and a sardine stone: and there was a rainbow round about the throne, in sight like unto an emerald.

[4] And round about the throne were four and twenty seats: and upon the seats I saw four and twenty elders sitting, clothed in white raiment; and they had on their heads crowns of gold.

[5] And out of the throne proceeded lightnings and thunderings and voices: and there were seven lamps

of fire burning before the throne, which are the seven Spirits of God.

⁶ And before the throne there was a sea of glass like unto crystal: and in the midst of the throne, and round about the throne, were four beasts full of eyes before and behind.

⁷ And the first beast was like a lion, and the second beast like a calf, and the third beast had a face as a man, and the fourth beast was like a flying eagle.

⁸ And the four beasts had each of them six wings about him; and they were full of eyes within: and they rest not day and night, saying, Holy, holy, holy, Lord God Almighty, which was, and is, and is to come.

⁹ And when those beasts give glory and honour and thanks to him that sat on the throne, who liveth for ever and ever,

¹⁰ The four and twenty elders fall down before him that sat on the throne, and worship him that liveth for ever and ever, and cast their crowns before the throne, saying,

The Message Version

4 Then I looked, and, oh!—a door open into Heaven. The trumpet-voice, the first voice in my vision, called out, "Ascend and enter. I'll show you what happens next."

²⁻⁶ I was caught up at once in deep worship and, oh!—a Throne set in Heaven with One Seated on the Throne, suffused in gem hues of amber and flame with a nimbus of emerald. Twenty-four thrones circled the Throne, with Twenty-four Elders seated, white-robed, gold-crowned. Lightning flash and thunder crash pulsed from the Throne. Seven fire-blazing torches fronted the Throne (these are the Sevenfold Spirit of God). Before the Throne it was like a clear crystal sea.

⁶⁻⁸ Prowling around the Throne were Four Animals, all eyes. Eyes to look ahead, eyes to look behind. The first Animal like a lion, the second like an ox, the third with a human face, the fourth like an eagle in flight. The Four Animals were winged, each with six wings. They were all eyes, seeing around and within. And they chanted night and day, never taking a break:

Holy, holy, holy
Is God our Master, Sovereign-Strong,
THE WAS, THE IS, THE COMING.

Weapon Thirty Seven

CLAPPING is to strike the palm of ones hands together repeatedly typically in order to applaud or to show approval.

Psalm 47:1
O clap your hands, all ye people; shout unto God with the voice of triumph.

There is even an anointing in your hand clap, it is noise that disturbs the enemy. It say, "Well done Father, I salute you."

Weapon Thirty Eight

Shouting a loud vocal expression of strong emotion

Joshua 6:2-16; 20-21

² And the LORD said unto Joshua, See, I have given into thine hand Jericho, and the king thereof, and the mighty men of valour.

³ And ye shall compass the city, all ye men of war, and go round about the city once. Thus shalt thou do six days.

⁴ And <u>seven priests</u> shall bear before the ark <u>seven trumpets</u> of rams' horns: and the <u>seventh day</u> ye shall <u>compass the city seven times</u>, and the priests shall blow with the trumpets.

⁵ And it shall come to pass, that when they make a long blast with the ram's horn, and when ye hear the sound of the trumpet, all the people shall **shout** with a great **shout**; and the wall of the city shall fall down flat, and the people shall ascend up every man straight before him.

⁶ And Joshua the son of Nun called the priests, and said unto them, Take up the ark of the covenant, and let seven priests bear seven trumpets of rams' horns before the ark of the LORD.

⁷ And he said unto the people, Pass on, and compass the city, and let him that is armed pass on before the ark of the Lord.

⁸ And it came to pass, when Joshua had spoken unto the people, that the seven priests bearing the seven trumpets of rams' horns passed on before the Lord, and blew with the trumpets: and the ark of the covenant of the Lord followed them.

⁹ And the armed men went before the priests that blew with the trumpets, and the re-reward came after the ark, the priests going on, and blowing with the trumpets. (rear guard)

¹⁰ And Joshua had commanded the people, saying, Ye shall not shout, nor make any noise with your voice, neither shall any word proceed out of your mouth, until the day I bid you shout; then shall ye shout.

¹¹ So the ark of the Lord compassed the city, going about it once: and they came into the camp, and lodged in the camp.

¹² And Joshua rose early in the morning, and the priests took up the ark of the Lord.

¹³ And seven priests bearing seven trumpets of rams' horns before the ark of the Lord went on continually, and blew with the trumpets: and the armed men went before them; but the re-reward came after the ark of the Lord, the priests going on, and blowing with the trumpets.

¹⁴ And <u>the second day they compassed the city once</u>, and returned into the camp: <u>so they did six days</u>.

¹⁵ And it came to pass <u>on the seventh day</u>, that they rose early about the dawning of the day, and compassed the city after the same manner seven times: only on that day they compassed the city seven times.

(13 times) The number 13 is a number of great blessings given by God. (At 99 years old, God's Promise came to Abraham, it was 13 years between the promise given and the Promise manifested.

¹⁶ And it came to pass at the seventh time, when the priests blew with the trumpets, Joshua said unto the people, Shout; for the LORD hath given you the city.

²⁰ So the people **shouted** when the priests blew with the trumpets: and it came to pass, when the people heard the sound of the trumpet, and the people shouted with a great shout, that the wall fell down flat, so that the people went up into the city, every man straight before him, and they took the city.

²¹ And they utterly destroyed all that was in the city, both man and woman, young and old, and ox, and sheep, and ass, with the edge of the sword.

There are times when we need to be quiet so we can hear God, and there are times when we need to be quiet so that we can hear what the enemy is up to. There is much revelation when we listen to God and when we listen to others.

Weapon Thirty Nine

HALLEUJAH, is an expression of worship or rejoicing; an expression of joyful praise to God. It is the highest praise.

Revelation 19:1
And after these things I heard a great voice of much people in heaven, saying, Alleluia; Salvation, and glory, and honour, and power, unto the Lord our God:

Weapon Forty

Thanksgiving is the act of rendering thanks or expressing gratitude for favors or mercies.

1 Thessalonians 5:18
In every thing give thanks: for this is the will of God in Christ Jesus concerning you. A public celebration of divine goodness;

Ephesians 5:20
Giving thanks always for all things unto God and the Father in the name of our Lord Jesus Christ;

Philippians 4:6
Be careful for nothing; but in every thing by prayer and supplication with thanksgiving let your requests be made known unto God.

Psalm 107:1
O give thanks unto the Lord, for he is good: for his mercy endureth for ever.

In this day and time with the condition of the world, we can find so much to murmur and complain about, but the Lord has said to give thanks regardless of what it is, knowing that He will make it work for our good. God uses every experience to mature and perfect us.

Weapons of Maturity

Weapon Forty One

VISION a revelation from God; Something imagined to be seen, an appearance or exhibition of something supernaturally presented to the minds of the prophets/God's people

Proverbs 29:18
Where there is no vision, the people perish: but he that keepeth the law, happy is he.

Habakkuk 2:2
And the Lord answered me, and said, Write the vision, and make it plain upon tables, that he may run that readeth it.

We must be able to see our desire/dream before we can even write it down. If you can see it, if you can believe it, you can achieve it. Remembering that satan does not want us to see anything whether it be healing, deliverance, freedom, success, riches or happiness. He wants us to be blinded by his lies.

Weapon Forty Two

Writing the act or art of forming letters and characters, on paper, wood, stone or other material, for the purpose of recording the ideas which characters and the words express, or of communicating them to others by visible signs

Habakkuk 2:1-3
I will stand upon my watch, and set me upon the tower, and will watch to see what he will say unto me, and what I shall answer when I am reproved.

2 And the LORD answered me, and said, Write the vision, and make it plain upon tables, that he may run that readeth it.

3 For the vision is yet for an appointed time, but at the end it shall speak, and not lie: though it tarry, wait for it; because it will surely come, it will not tarry.

Isaiah 30:8
Now go, write it before them in a table, and note it in a book, that it may be for the time to come forever and ever:

Jeremiah 30:2
Thus speaketh the Lord God of Israel, saying, Write

thee all the words that I have spoken unto thee in a book.

When we write things down it gives life to it and we are more apt to move on it. When the enemy comes and tries to tell you this and that, you tell him "IT IS WRITTEN! Whether it be the Word of God or the faith in what you have written down concerning your desires, dreams and goals.

Weapon Forty Three

Focus a thing or place that is of greatest importance to an activity or interest, a guiding or motivating purpose or principle

Philippians 3:12-14
[12] Not as though I had already attained, either were already perfect: but I follow after, if that I may apprehend that for which also I am apprehended of Christ Jesus.

[13] Brethren, I count not myself to have apprehended: but this one thing I do, forgetting those things which are behind, and reaching forth unto those things which are before,

[14] I press toward the mark for the prize of the high calling of God in Christ Jesus.

Hebrews 12:1-3
Wherefore seeing we also are compassed about with so great a cloud of witnesses, let us lay aside every weight, and the sin which doth so easily beset us, and let us run with patience the race that is set before us,

[2] Looking unto Jesus the author and finisher of our faith; who for the joy that was set before him endured the cross, despising the shame, and is set down at the right hand of the throne of God.

Nehemiah 6:1-8

Now it came to pass when Sanballat, and Tobiah, and Geshem the Arabian, and the rest of our enemies, heard that I had builded the wall, and that there was no breach left therein; (though at that time I had not set up the doors upon the gates;)

² That Sanballat and Geshem sent unto me, saying, Come, let us meet together in some one of the villages in the plain of Ono. But they thought to do me mischief.

³ And I sent messengers unto them, saying, I am doing a great work, so that I cannot come down: why should the work cease, whilst I leave it, and come down to you?

⁴ Yet they sent unto me four times after this sort; and I answered them after the same manner.

⁵ Then sent Sanballat his servant unto me in like manner the fifth time with an open letter in his hand;

⁶ Wherein was written, It is reported among the heathen, and Gashmu saith it, that thou and the Jews think to rebel: for which cause thou buildest the wall, that thou mayest be their king, according to these words.

⁷ And thou hast also appointed prophets to preach of thee at Jerusalem, saying, There is a king in Judah: and now shall it be reported to the king according to these words. Come now therefore, and let us take counsel together.

⁸ Then I sent unto him, saying, There are no such things done as thou sayest, but thou feignest them out of thine own heart.

Satan will try any and everything to get you off focused, slow you up, and slow you down, to keep you from reaching your goal, your destiny. He uses his weapon called DISTRACTION. Therefore you must stay focused in this hour.

Weapon Forty Four

Determination a quality that makes you continue trying to do or achieve something that is difficult

Philippians 4:13
I can do all things through him who strengthens me.

Romans 15:4
For whatever was written in former days was written for our instruction, that through endurance and through the encouragement of the Scriptures we might have hope.

2 Timothy 4:7
I have fought a good fight, I have finished my course, I have kept the faith:

Paul had done everything he was supposed to do according to God's divine purpose for his life. That's why he could say this. What are you determined to do? Will you do it, will you complete it? The answer is yes, YES I WILL! Why? Because I am determined!

Weapon Forty Five

Persistence uninterrupted or lasting existence

Luke 1:1-8   The Message Version

[1-3] Jesus told them a story showing that it was necessary for them to pray consistently and never quit. He said, "There was once a judge in some city who never gave God a thought and cared nothing for people. A widow in that city kept after him: 'My rights are being violated. Protect me!'

[4-5] "He never gave her the time of day. But after this went on and on he said to himself, 'I care nothing what God thinks, even less what people think. But because this widow won't quit badgering me, I'd better do something and see that she gets justice—otherwise I'm going to end up beaten black-and-blue by her pounding.'"

[6-8] Then the Master said, "Do you hear what that judge, corrupt as he is, is saying? So what makes you think God won't step in and work justice for his chosen people, who continue to cry out for help? Won't he stick up for them? I assure you, he will. He will not drag his feet. But how much of that kind of persistent faith will the Son of Man find on the earth when he returns?"

1 Corinthians 15:57-58
But thanks be to God, which giveth us the victory through our Lord Jesus Christ. [58] Therefore, my beloved brethren, be ye stedfast, unmoveable, always abounding in the work of the Lord, forasmuch as ye know that your labour is not in vain in the Lord.

Don't give up, don't give out!

Weapon Forty Six

No refusal, will not comply, in no respect or degree

1 Corinthians 10:13
There hath no temptation taken you but such as is common to man: but God is faithful, who will not suffer you to be tempted above that ye are able; but will with the temptation also make a way to escape, that ye may be able to bear it.

The Message Version
No test or temptation that comes your way is beyond the course of what others have had to face. All you need to remember is that God will never let you down; he'll never let you be pushed past your limit; he'll always be there to help you come through it.

When we are tempted by the enemy to say and do things we know are not of God, in line with his will the answer is NO!

Weapons of the Pocketbook

Weapon Forty Seven

Tithing the tenth part of one's income that's owed to God

Malachi 3:10-11
[10] Bring ye all the tithes into the storehouse, that there may be meat in mine house, and prove me now herewith, saith the Lord of hosts, if I will not open you the windows of heaven, and pour you out a blessing, that there shall not be room enough to receive it.

[11] And I will rebuke the devourer for your sakes, and he shall not destroy the fruits of your ground; neither shall your vine cast her fruit before the time in the field, saith the Lord of hosts.

Tithing is like putting money in the bank, when you need it you can go and withdraw it out. The Father makes sure your needs are met, that you will not do without or skip a beat.

Weapon Forty Eight

Sowing is a spiritual law and it relates to seed sown in two primary areas, one is the Word of God and the second is finance. The scriptures speak mostly about finance when it relates to sowing. Sowing also relates to multiplication because the seed sown will be multiplied rather than duplicated. When we sow the Word of God, the hearer should and will produce faith and maturity. Sowing will always produce whether good or evil. When you sow there will always be a harvest.

Proverbs 3:9-10 Common English Bible
Honor the Lord with your wealth, with the firstfruits of all your crops; then your barns will be filled to overflowing, and your vats will brim over with new wine,"

Proverbs 10:22 New Century Version
The Lord's blessing brings wealth, and no sorrow comes with it.

Luke 6:38
Give, and it shall be given unto you; good measure, pressed down, and shaken together, and running over, shall men give into your bosom. For with the same measure that ye mete withal it shall be measured to you again.

2 Corinthians 9:6-7

⁶ But this I say, He which soweth sparingly shall reap also sparingly; and he which soweth bountifully shall reap also bountifully.

⁷ Every man according as he purposeth in his heart, so let him give; not grudgingly, or of necessity: for God loveth a cheerful giver.

1 Kings 17:8-16

⁸ And the word of the Lord came unto him, saying,

⁹ Arise, get thee to Zarephath, which belongeth to Zidon, and dwell there: behold, I have commanded a widow woman there to sustain thee.

¹⁰ So he arose and went to Zarephath. And when he came to the gate of the city, behold, the widow woman was there gathering of sticks: and he called to her, and said, Fetch me, I pray thee, a little water in a vessel, that I may drink.

¹¹ And as she was going to fetch it, he called to her, and said, Bring me, I pray thee, a morsel of bread in thine hand.

¹² And she said, As the Lord thy God liveth, I have not a cake, but an handful of meal in a barrel, and a little oil in a cruse: and, behold, I am gathering two sticks, that I may go in and dress it for me and my son, that we may eat it, and die.

¹³ And Elijah said unto her, Fear not; go and do as thou hast said: but make me thereof a little cake

first, and bring it unto me, and after make for thee and for thy son.

[14] For thus saith the LORD God of Israel, The barrel of meal shall not waste, neither shall the cruse of oil fail, until the day that the LORD sendeth rain upon the earth.

[15] And she went and did according to the saying of Elijah: and she, and he, and her house, did eat many days.

[16] And the barrel of meal wasted not, neither did the cruse of oil fail, according to the word of the LORD, which he spake by Elijah.

If you want to be blessed give, take Him at His Word, bring it back to His remembrance and watch Him show out

Final Weapon

Weapon Forty Nine

Rest is a peace of mind or spirit knowing God is in control.

Matthew 11:28-30
28 Come unto me, all ye that labour and are heavy laden, and I will give you rest.

29 Take my yoke upon you, and learn of me; for I am meek and lowly in heart: and ye shall find rest unto your souls.

30 For my yoke is easy, and my burden is light.

The Message Version
28-30 "Are you tired? Worn out? Burned out on religion? Come to me. Get away with me and you'll recover your life. I'll show you how to take a real rest. Walk with me and work with me—watch how I do it. Learn the unforced rhythms of grace. I won't lay anything heavy or ill-fitting on you. Keep company with me and you'll learn to live freely and lightly."

Mark 6:31   (21st Century King James Version)
31 And He said unto them, "Come ye yourselves apart into a desert place, and rest a while." For there were many coming and going, and they had no leisure, even so much as to eat.

Exodus 34:21
Do your work in six days and rest on the seventh day, even during the seasons for plowing and harvesting.

In this hour not only do we need to learn to get our physical rest, we must also learn how to stop being stressed about things we have no control over. We are to cast all our care upon Him who cares for you.

Be quick to give it to God and let Him/All wise/All knowing/All powerful/Omni present, take care of things we can't fix. We sing the song "Jesus Will Fix It" then let him do it, **REST!**

Rest in everything that you have read in this book; knowing that you have forty nine weapons to use against the enemy. Knowing that if you operate in the first one which is obedience, everything else will fall in place. It worked for Job and it will work for you.

A List of the Enemy's Weapon

Weapons of the Enemy

1. Deception
2. Lies
3. Distraction
4. Old Nature/Flesh
5. Lust
6. Enticement
7. Allurement
8. Seducing
9. Fornication
10. Adultery
11. Pride
12. Arrogance
13. FEAR
14. Self-exaltation
15. Frustration
16. Anger
17. Rage
18. Provoking
19. Disobedience
20. Jealousy

21. Rebellion
22. Murder
23. Witchcraft
24. Gossip
25. Division
26. Sickness
27. Depression
28. Thievery
29. Double mindedness
30. Murmuring
31. Complaining
32. Unthankful/Ungrateful
33. Confusion
34. Slothfulness/Laziness
35. Intimidation
36. Low self esteem
37. Ignorance
38. Lack
39. Gluttony
40. Embarrassment
41. Torment
42. Suicide

About the Author

Dr. Ruth M. Wilson is the Pastor and Founder of the Shekinah Glory International Ministries located in Louisville, KY. She is on a personal mission to expose the enemy for who and what he is; a LIAR and a THIEF.

She believes that once we know the truth we can't help but be free.

"And ye shall know the truth, and the truth shall make you free." John 8:32 (KJV)

God is not a respecter of persons. What He does for one, He will do for another; He'll do it for you.

It is our prayer that this book has been an eye opener, life, and motivation for you to know the weapons that you possess and how to use them against the enemy.

Dr. Wilson is available to speak at workshops, conferences, revivals, all media interviews and can be contacted via the information below.

Let us know, tell someone else or if you would like to order additional copies send all correspondence to:

Dr. Ruth Wilson
P. O. Box 133
Louisville, KY 40201
Email us at: dauparoom@yahoo.com

www.ingramcontent.com/pod-product-compliance
Lightning Source LLC
Chambersburg PA
CBHW051933160426
43198CB00012B/2130